Columbia University

Contributions to Education

Teachers College Series

No. 856

AMS PRESS
NEW YORK

YOUTH

AND

INSTRUCTION IN MARRIAGE

AND FAMILY LIVING

BY

LAURA WINSLOW DRUMMOND

Submitted in Partial Fulfillment of
the Requirements for the Degree of Doctor
of Philosophy in the Faculty of Philosophy
Columbia University

Published with the Approval of
Professor HELEN JUDY-BOND, *Sponsor*

BUREAU OF PUBLICATIONS
TEACHERS COLLEGE, COLUMBIA UNIVERSITY
NEW YORK, 1942

Library of Congress Cataloging in Publication Data

Drummond, Laura Winslow, 1901-1961.
    Youth and instruction in marriage and family living.

    Reprint of the 1942 ed., issued in series: Teachers
College, Columbia University. Contributions to educa-
tion, no. 856.
    Originally presented as the author's thesis, Columbia.
    Bibliography: p.
    1. Family life education. I. Title. II. Series:
Columbia University. Teachers College. Contributions to
education, no. 856
HQ10.D76 1972   301.41'8'07   74-176731
ISBN 0-404-55856-9

Reprinted by Special Arrangement with Teachers
College Press, New York, New York

From the edition of 1942, New York
First AMS edition published in 1972
Manufactured in the United States

AMS PRESS, INC.
NEW YORK, N. Y.   10003

Acknowledgments

To Professor Helen Judy-Bond and Professor Maurice A. Bigelow the author wishes to express her appreciation for counsel so generously given in the initiation and conduct of this study. The thoughtful guidance of the members of the dissertation committee, Professors Helen Judy-Bond, Lyman Bryson, and Helen M. Walker, is acknowledged with sincere gratitude.

Those persons who made it possible to secure the cooperation of undergraduate students and alumni at the two institutions gave invaluable assistance. The interest and encouragement of staff members in the department of Household Arts and Sciences at Teachers College and the able assistance of Miriam Ruth Tyler and Robert E. Dengler are deeply appreciated.

LAURA W. DRUMMOND

Contents

YOUTH

AND
INSTRUCTION IN MARRIAGE
AND FAMILY LIVING

I:
Summary

In AMERICAN colleges and universities during the last decade, the amount of instruction dealing with the family has increased rapidly. The trend is toward greater emphasis on modern problems of family adjustment, and the practical and personal needs of youth are receiving more attention than ever before. This study attempts to discover what young people themselves consider important materials of instruction with regard to marriage and the family.

A questionnaire soliciting anonymous free response suggestions, a personal data form, and a check list of questions proposed for discussion were developed. These were presented in regularly scheduled class periods to undergraduate men and women majoring in liberal arts in two large Pennsylvania universities. Comparable forms were mailed at intervals to alumni of one to five years' standing. Responses were received from 320 freshmen, 164 seniors, and 148 alumni.

Sociological data reported by the participants were analyzed to discover significant variation in selected background traits between men and women, and between those from the two colleges and between the several classes. These findings are summarized on pages 29 and 31. Because of the possible implications which the findings might have in curriculum planning for youth groups differing in age, sex, and home and community background, the following population sub-groups were defined: college "S" and college "T"; freshmen, seniors, and alumni; men and women; single, engaged, and married persons; and those rating their family life ideal, successful-satisfactory, and indifferent-unsatisfactory. The value ratings given to questions on the check list and the distribution of written suggestions among categories describing areas of concern were analyzed, using the Chi-Square Test of significance and analysis of variance.

1

Many of the suggestions revealed acute personal problems and re-flected the actual family situations described on the personal data form. The responses appeared to be frank and sincere. Freshmen frequently used the first person and discussed immediate personal conflicts, whereas seniors and alumni tended to state their suggestions in more general and impersonal terms. Although the emphasis and method of expression varied from group to group, many of the same topics and questions were proposed by all groups.

A total of 2,752 suggestions concerning instruction in marriage and the family were received. Approximately one suggestion in four dealt with sex. These young people asked for specific information about premarital and marital sex adjustments. Other areas of concern, in descending order of frequency, were premarriage problems including dating, courtship, and choice of mate; accord in marriage and family relationships; family economics with special reference to budgeting; child guidance and the role of the child in the family; adjustments between generations; discord; religion in family living; and the family as a social institution.*

In the distribution of suggestions among selected areas, significant differences were found between the two universities, between freshmen and seniors, and between seniors and alumni. The findings in Chapter V show that, in terms of distribution of response, freshmen and seniors were more similar than seniors and alumni. Men and women varied little in the type and frequency of their proposals for instruction in marriage and family living.

Written suggestions in certain areas did not appear to be related, quantitatively, to differences in family income and place of abode. No evidence of association was discovered between the level of family income and the frequency of suggestions on family economics. Whether a person lived with his family or away from home did not appear to be associated with the number of suggestions dealing with adjustments between generations. However, those who had had some instruction in sociology tended to give more suggestions dealing with the family as an institution than those who had not studied in this field.

* See pages 109–112 for further analysis of the relative emphasis among categories.

Although the check list revealed less variation in response between sub-groups of participants than the written suggestions, the direction of variation was consistent. The findings reported in Chapter VI show that questions dealing with sex and premarriage problems were generally rated much more valuable for discussion than those dealing with religion or the family as a social institution. Participants from the two colleges rated the questions on the check list very much alike. The questions dealing with birth control and marital adjustments seemed more valuable to seniors than to either freshmen or alumni. Whereas freshmen and seniors agreed on the relative value of most of the questions proposed for discussion, seniors and alumni differed significantly on more than half of them. Seniors tended to consider these more valuable than alumni.

Although men and women varied little in their estimates of the relative value of questions for discussion, two questions received significantly different ratings. These were courtship adjustments, and marriage versus career. Women considered these more important for discussion than did men. Marriage and plans for marriage seemed to be associated with value ratings on only three questions. These dealt with being popular, with opposing parents, and with religious differences as a hazard to successful marriage. These seemed more important to unmarried young persons than to those who were married or engaged.

The person's satisfaction with his own family life seemed to have little association with his rating of specific questions dealing with family problems. In contrast with the written suggestions (page 120), the check list ratings (page 141) failed to reveal significant differences in areas of concern between those who varied markedly in their ratings of present family life. Those participants, however, whose parents were separated or divorced considered the question of divorce more valuable for discussion than those who came from unbroken homes. Students who had had no instruction in sociology rated the question on divorce more important than those who had taken sociology courses.

No evidence of association was found between the evaluation of check list questions on adjustments between generations and the fact that the person did or did not live with his family. The rating of questions on family economics varied little between those whose mothers were full-time homemakers and those whose mothers were employed outside the home. Nor did estimated family income appear to be associated with the rating of questions on family economics. These findings reported on pages 146 and 147 are consistent with those obtained through the analysis of the written suggestions summarized on pages 122–123 and 124.

CONCLUSIONS

Young people believe that instruction in marriage and family living is highly desirable. When given an opportunity to suggest what they believe are important problems and questions for consideration in such instruction, young men and women respond eagerly and constructively. Their recommendations tend to center around problems of human relations rather than material resources. They ask for a realistic consideration of sex, premarriage problems, accord in family relationships, and family economics. Children in the family and adjustments between generations are of moderate concern, while there appears to be relatively little interest in family discord, religion, and the family as an institution.

In this study freshmen and seniors tended to agree in areas considered important for discussion, although seniors emphasized marital adjustments more often and freshmen stressed choice of mate, courtship, and dating. Areas of concern varied significantly between participants from the two colleges represented. The sex of the participant seemed of little import; men and women subjects showed marked similarity of response.

IMPLICATIONS

In developing a functional program of instruction in marriage and family living the recommendations of young people themselves should be utilized. Such instruction should take into account the areas of greatest and least importance as expressed by the particular group concerned.

Admission to study groups and classes in marriage and family life should be based on the need and readiness of the person rather than on his college class or chronological age.

Discussion leaders and teachers in the field of education for marriage and family living should be familiar with the resources and recent findings in many related fields, such as the biological and physical sciences, psychology, economics, sociology, philosophy, and home economics.

Effective education for marriage and family living is a function of the college as a whole.

The wide range of acute concerns among individuals in any large group indicates a need for a personal counseling service open to all.

In planning the freshman orientation program, perplexities of first-year students with regard to family adjustments and preparation for marriage should be considered.

Adult classes and discussion groups dealing with marriage and family living should be available to adults in the community.

2:

The Development of Education for Marriage and Family Living

O NLY recently has education for marriage and family living been recognized as a function of the school. Just as the home has shared with other social agencies many of its economic and protective functions, it is now gradually transferring to the school part of its responsibility for education for marriage and family living. Educators agree that family life experience is extremely powerful in developing personality and in shaping lasting patterns of human relationships. "The home is literally the nursery of humanity, the matrix of personality during the most impressionable years, and a continuing influence throughout life. To what degree a person is fearful, ruthless or reasonable, bigoted and autocratic, or tolerant and democratic is perhaps determined more completely by relations in early family life than by any other set of experiences. Not only are those experiences first in time and prepotent in effect during childhood, but family relationships continuously influence the manner in which persons conduct their affairs in other groups. One important responsibility of education, therefore, is to improve and develop home and family life." [13 : 80] *

Clear-cut evidence of the growing concern of youth, educators, and community leaders with preparation for marriage and family life became apparent in the period of economic depression following 1930. The need for conserving and promoting human values in marriage and family life in a world of stress and strain stirred diverse groups to action. In 1934 a Conference on Education for Marriage and Family Social Relations, sponsored by Teachers College, the American Social Hygiene Association, and the American Home Economics Associa-

* Throughout the book figures in brackets indicate number of references listed in Bibliography, pages 159–160.

tion, was held at Columbia University to pool the thinking and resources of social workers, religious leaders, physicians, home economists,
sociologists, and laymen in a direct attempt to stimulate more effective
preparation for marriage and family living. An outgrowth of this
meeting was the organization in 1938 of The National Conference on
Family Relations to include all persons and agencies working for the
promotion of family relations. Affiliated state and regional conferences
have since been organized in many communities. [30]

In 1937 the demands of young men and women in a number of colleges throughout the country for instruction in marriage and family
living were crystallized in the action of the American Youth Congress
in support of marriage courses. Leaders of young people sought special
training in how to teach these courses. Schools, colleges, and community organizations experimented with various methods and types of
instruction. The decade between 1930 and 1940 witnessed an awaken-
ing to the realization that education for marriage and family living
could make a significant contribution to individual happiness and
social welfare.

SOME FACTORS STIMULATING INTEREST IN EDUCATION FOR MARRIAGE AND FAMILY LIVING

The increasing appreciation that childhood experiences are significant
in personal adjustment, effective group participation, and successful
marriage is a major factor in the growing concern with family education. Children bring to nursery school and kindergarten not only certain reserves of health and habits but also clearly defined values and
persistent patterns of behavior. The emotional stability of the young
child and adolescent is largely a product of the home. Parents have a
unique opportunity to help build stable, well-adjusted adults for the
unpredictable world of today and tomorrow. They hold the key position in laying foundations for success in their children's marriages.
That the happiness of parents is positively associated with the marital
adjustment of their children is shown by two recent studies of marital
happiness. [10, 26] Parents and prospective parents, therefore, have
reason to be concerned with education for family living.

Community leaders are recognizing the importance of family life

experience in developing attitudes, values, and techniques of cooperation needed for effective social action. The ability to adjust oneself in
group living outside the home appears to be conditioned by the family
life experiences of children and adults. In studying cases of pupils
who are considered problem children at school, teachers often find a
history of unsatisfactory family relationships; and high school counselors and college deans find that satisfying family life is related to
success in academic work. The conclusion reached by one investigator, after a series of controlled interviews with several hundred college students, is that "campus adjustment and home adjustment seem
to be positively correlated." [2] Industrial leaders, who have learned
through experience in selecting young men for responsible positions
that happy marriage is a valuable asset, believe they have evidence to
show association between vocational efficiency and family life adjustment. Therefore, teachers, employers, and community leaders are
interested in the relation of family life adjustment and success in group
living outside the home, for they have much to gain if education for
marriage and family living can be made more effective.

The influence on the family of new conditions in contemporary
culture stimulates much concern with family adjustment, as rapidly
changing ways of life throw into high relief the difficulty of trying to
apply to new conditions old patterns and values in family living.
Young persons mature in a very different world from that which accepted their parents and grandparents as adults. Each year two million
boys and girls reach the biological age for marriage. Many are physio-
logically, psychologically, and emotionally mature, yet continue to be
economically dependent and subject to parental control. The opportunity to assume such adult responsibilities as earning a living,
owning property, founding a home, and rearing children is denied,
yet society still measures success in terms of economic independence.
"The patterns for this older way of life remain, but the social-economic
situation to which they were addressed is altered. Young men and
women face either frustration in their efforts to conform to the older
patterns or confusion and anxiety as they explore for new patterns of
conduct. These frustrations and anxieties are the dominant aspect of
home and family life today." [16 : 98]

The disjunction between culture patterns and economic pressures as they affect family living is making people more thoughtful about preparation for marriage. Youth, as they attempt to establish economic independence in an era of unprecedented unemployment, are faced by overwhelming difficulties. The prolonged dependence of boys and young men and the frustration of ambition are painful in a culture that still places a premium on male dominance measured in terms of wage earning. Delayed marriage for the boy frequently means a longer period of employment for the single girl, and the attendant freedom and financial independence make it more difficult for her to adjust wants and needs to the level warranted by the modest earnings of the young man. Many a husband feels that it is a reflection on his ability and manliness for the wife to earn outside the home. Responsibilities to support aging parents and to resolve college debts are often incompatible with the kind of living which the girl and man desire. The social approval given to establishing an independent household is in continual conflict with the necessity of stretching one roof to cover several families. Parents and youth have reason to be concerned with education for marriage in a world of such basic inconsistencies.

Perhaps in no area of human experience is the contrast between the old and the new so sharp as in attitudes toward sex. Advisers of young people report that many boys and girls accept physical intimacies as both natural and honorable. Spontaneous demonstrations of affection, such as kissing, petting, and "pitching woo," are sanctioned upon short acquaintance. Full and specific information about sex is generally accepted as the privilege of youth: they demand their right to know the facts.

The older generation often looks askance at these changing attitudes and standards. Bromley and Britten [8] believe that many parents dare not impose strict standards for they are afraid of the subject of sex. Rather, they merely let it be known in a general way that they expect their children always to do the right thing. Then trouble comes in defining the right thing because parents and children often base discussions and judgments on quite different values. For instance, Baber [4] found that college students and their parents were far apart in their ideas on moral standards expected in a prospective mate. Parents insisted more strongly than did their sons and daughters that the latter should not marry a person with lower moral standards.

Folsom [14 : 401] reports a trend among college youth in the period between 1930 and 1940 toward a more conservative and responsible attitude with regard to sexual experimentation than was evident in the preceding decade. Another writer [21] in the field suggests that attitudes toward sex and marriage probably have changed more than the behavior itself.

The rapid change in attitude with regard to sex has made many parents and young people welcome a program of sex education in the schools. Parents often lack both the knowledge and the emotional stability needed for acceptance of full responsibility for the preparation of boys and girls for the physical, psychological, and emotional aspects of mate-seeking and marriage. Parents, sons, and daughters are turning more often to the secondary school for frank discussions of sex and for private conferences on personal problems. Colleges, too, are being forced to accept more responsibility for sex education. "Taken as a group, college men and women are more conscious of their needs and more willing to face their emotional conflicts than are most youth. The institution of higher learning that accepts the responsibility of preparing these men and women for life cannot, in fairness, ignore the sex part of the student's life, since it influences campus success and later adult character. . . . Not only is it sound educational policy to attempt to furnish youth, who are later likely to become social leaders, with a background that will help them make their own marriages a success, but there is also the advantage of maturing and intellectualizing the sex interest that is usually at flood tide." [18 : 358]

Changing points of view with regard to mate selection and the role of the wife and child in the home have stimulated more general acceptance of family life education as a function of the school. Although their actions sometimes belie their words, young people challenge the traditions of romantic courtship and of male aggression in mate-seeking. Mate selection is less likely to be romanticized, for it is fashionable to claim that marriage will be a matter not of the heart but of the head. Boys and girls are asking for the results of studies that give facts rather than opinion on questions of dating, courtship, and marriage.

Another factor arousing concern with family education in school is the prolonged periods when children are away from parental guidance and control. With child and parent separated for many hours of each day, careful supervision by parents is no longer possible. Children and youth must make many of their own decisions and accept more direct responsibility for their own actions. Parents look to the school to help develop standards and values to guide these actions and decisions.

The changing role of the wife as a contributor to the family income has intensified certain emotional conflicts for both youth and adults. Approximately one-fourth of the wage earners of the country are women, and at least one-third of these women are engaged in homemaking as well as in gainful employment. An understanding of the economic aspects of family living is being demanded as a direct contribution of the school to preparation for marriage.

The growing conviction that the duration of marriage is a matter of choice emphasizes rational as well as spiritual and emotional controls in the marriage relationship. Although many people favor reduction in the cost and trouble of divorce proceedings, few actually want a divorce. That increasing ease in terminating marriage gives youth courage to face the uncertainties of marriage is a statement on which opinions vary, but certainly this very ease is a potent factor in the deliberations of youth.

These changing values in family relationships and contemporary life give impetus to the sharing of responsibility by home and school in preparation of youth for marriage or family life.

AGENCIES INTERESTED IN FAMILY EDUCATION

The widespread concern with education for marriage and family living is reflected in the expanding activities of local, state, and national groups in this field. Many organizations and agencies devote part of their programs to family education. Churches and religious groups were among the first to attempt a direct program to prepare young men and women for marriage. The Roman Catholic Church has taken much responsibility for individual and group instruction of both youth and adults, and many Protestants and Jewish groups sponsor programs and series of conferences on family adjustments and boy-girl relationships. The Committee on Marriage and the Home, of the Federal Council of Churches of Christ in America, is especially interested in preparation for marriage. Organizations sponsored by groups such as the Young Men's Christian Association, Young Women's Christian Association, Young Hebrew Association, and the Sodalities have well-defined programs designed to help their members understand the complex interplay of relations in the family group and their roles in present and future families. In their stated purposes and in many local programs, the Girl Scouts, Boy Scouts, Camp Fire Girls, 4-H Clubs, Junior Grange, and other organizations serving teen age boys and girls give official recognition to the importance of family life education.

Many lay and professional organizations direct part of their program toward education for marriage and family living. Among them are the General Federation of Women's Clubs, the National Grange, the National Congress of Parents and Teachers, the American Association of University Women, the National Council of Parent Education, the Child Study Association of America, the American Social Hygiene Association, the National Council on Family Relations, the American Home Economics Association, the Youth Commission of the American Council on Education, the Commission on Human Relations of the Progressive Education Association, and the American Association for Adult Education. The Merrill Palmer School, the Vassar Institute of Euthenics, and the Annual Conference on Conservation of Marriage and the Family sponsored by the University of North Carolina have pioneered in training lay and professional leaders for these groups. The 1941 Yearbook of the American Association of School Administrators entitled "Education for Family Life," [1] and the report on "Family Living and Our Schools" prepared by a committee of experts representing the Society for Curriculum Study and the Department of Home Economics of the National Education Association [17] provide evidence of the concern of educators in this field. The interest of the United States government in family education is expressed primarily through projects and publications of the Office of Education, the Bureau of Home Economics, the Home Economics Extension Service, Women's Bureau, Children's Bureau, the National Youth Administration, and the Farm Security Administration. The Institute of Family Relations in Los Angeles and the Marriage Council in Philadelphia are outstanding examples of private family consultation bureaus which provide expert counseling on most types of family problems while carrying on a positive program of education for marriage. The number of organizations and agencies with clearly defined programs of family education is increasing steadily, and the diversity of their programs is as striking as their rapid growth.

THE COLLEGE AND EDUCATION FOR MARRIAGE

Until recently colleges and universities played a relatively limited role in the nation-wide trend toward providing more functional education for marriage and family living. In a study (unpublished) dated 1926 Wells [28] found that 15 colleges as early as 1920 offered instruction in family relations, with only four of the courses initiated prior to 1910. A later study [20] reports 22 courses in this field in 1923. Wells found descriptions of courses in the family in the 1925–26 catalogues of 45, or approximately one-fourth, of the 187 institutions accredited by the American Association of Colleges. Most of the courses were called "The Family," carried two to three credits, were open to juniors and seniors who had completed an introductory course in sociology, and emphasized the history of the family and family disorganization. The textbook most frequently used was Goodsell's *History of the Family*.

In 1932 the White House Conference on Child Health and Protection assembled information on pre-parental education in 269 accredited institutions of higher education and reported courses on the family in 52 colleges, or approximately one-third of the institutions replying to the inquiry. [29] Thirty-nine of the colleges were coeducational; 11 were women's colleges and two were men's colleges. Some of these institutions indicated growing emphasis on preparation for marriage, parenthood, and family life. A course called "Marriage," which attracted much attention at the time, was first offered in 1926 as an elective course at the University of North Carolina. This course, taken for credit by over 100 men each year, was especially popular with pre-medical and pre-legal students. The instructor, Professor E. R. Groves, a sociologist with experience in biology, psychiatry, child study, and parent education, handled the course on an informal lecture-discussion basis with emphasis on practical problems of marriage and family adjustment, and supplemented classroom instruction with many individual conferences.

The trend away from lectures limited to theoretical aspects of the family as a social institution toward greater consideration of contemporary problems gained momentum slowly, although the number of courses dealing with the family multiplied rapidly. In a study of the 1933–35 official catalogues of 403 institutions belonging to the Association of American Colleges, Haworth [20] found courses in the family offered by 225 colleges. His findings are consistent with those of Wells in that many more women's colleges than men's colleges offered instruction in this field. Approximately two out of every three coeducational and women's colleges offered at least one course in the family, as contrasted with fewer than one in three of the men's colleges. Eighty per cent of the courses were sponsored by departments of sociology. The distribution of time to the discussion of 24 topics submitted to instructors of 105 courses indicated primary emphasis on social theory. Only one of the five high ranking topics dealt with personal adjustments in marriage. A median enrollment of 24 students indicates that a very small part of the population in these institutions was being reached by the instruction in 1935.

In September, 1933, an inquiry concerning instruction in family relations was addressed to the heads of home economics departments by the American Home Economics Association. [12] Of the 245 institutions replying 189 offered a separate course in family relations in the home economics department, and 65 offered a separate course on the family in the sociology or social science departments. These data supplement the findings of a questionnaire study sponsored by the Office of Education in 1930. [22] Responses were received from 555 of the 1,350 institutions of higher education on the mailing list. Courses on the family were found in 283 colleges and universities; 56 per cent of the courses were in departments of home economics. The large proportion of these courses sponsored by home economists may be associated with the fact that the data were collected as part of a study of home economics offerings. One college generation later an independent survey, made by Bigelow and Judy-Bond [7], of 250 colleges known to be developing courses on the family, revealed a relatively small proportion of the instruction listed under departments of home economics. Three out of every four courses in the family in 192 colleges were offered either by departments of sociology or by departments of social science.

An unpublished study directed by Professor Maurice A. Bigelow and sponsored by the Institute of Practical Science Research, Teachers College, Columbia University, showed that approximately one-third of the catalogues of the 487 accredited colleges and universities listed in the 1936 United States Directory offered courses on the family or family social relations. In April, 1936, an inquiry was addressed to the 487 institutions of higher education to obtain further information concerning work in this field. Two hundred and one colleges responded; 166 of these indicated that they offered instruction in marriage and family social relations which constituted the major part of the course reported. Seventy-two per cent of the colleges reporting instruction were coeducational; 20 per cent were women's colleges; and only 8 per cent were men's colleges. As in the Haworth study [20] made in the previous year, it was found that courses in the family were more frequently sponsored by sociologists than by any other group. Seventy-one per cent of all courses reported were offered by the social science departments, 22 per cent by the home economics departments, and 6 per cent by the departments of psychology, religion, philosophy, and zoology.

Differences of opinion as to the major purpose of the instruction were striking. Sixty-three instructors of the courses offered through social science departments checked the statement "to make a scientific study of the family from one or more of the following points of view: historical, sociological, psychological." Many of them underscored the words historical and sociological. The primary purpose of another 59 instructors in social science was indicated as follows: "To help individuals both married and unmarried make more satisfying adjustments to the everyday problems of family living." Thirty-four home economists checked personal adjustment as the primary purpose of the instruction as contrasted to only five who checked the scientific study of the family. The fact that these purposes are not mutually exclusive should be recognized in interpreting these data. However, the greater emphasis placed on relationships by the home economists is self-evident. One leader in the field states: "It is a notable fact that schools and departments of home economics now lay a great deal of stress upon family relationships." [3 : 618]

Men were enrolled in five of the 43 home economics courses reported to the Institute of Practical Science Research. Five out of every six courses sponsored by departments of home economics included students majoring in other fields. In 26 of the 130 courses in coeducational colleges women only were enrolled, yet in 18 of the remaining 104 coeducational courses the number of men enrolled exceeded the number of women. Courses serving men only tended to have a larger total enrollment than courses serving women only. The average number enrolled were 50 and 32 respectively. The mean enrollment in courses including both men and women students was 47, with the approximate ratio of two women to every man. Apparently courses in marriage and the family attracted many more students in 1936 than in the previous year, as reported by Haworth.

In 65 per cent of the colleges reporting to the Institute of Practical Science Research in the Spring of 1936, the enrollment was restricted to juniors and seniors. Only one course in twelve was open to freshmen. First and second year students frequently were excluded from courses on the family because of the prerequisites. Two-thirds of the prerequisite courses carried the equivalent of three or more semester hours credit. Some instructors volunteered information that crowded curricula limited to a large extent the opportunity for many students to elect these courses and subsequent courses dealing with marriage and the family.

Some indication of a trend toward the participation of specialists other than the regular instructor was observed in reports from certain colleges, although this was not true in approximately two-thirds of the courses. The number of specialists participating in any one course ranged from one to thirteen, while the average number used in 57 courses was two. However, 15 courses used four or more persons from other fields. The fields most frequently represented by specialists were social work 27, sociology 17, home economics 17, medicine 16, and religion 15. Several courses appeared to be cooperative projects where the participating specialists helped to plan and evaluate the entire course. The following courses reported in 1936 illustrate the diversity in title and leadership as well as in the number of specialists used.

College	Title of Course	In Charge	Number of Specialists
Boston University, Mass.	Psychology and the Family	Psychology Department	7
Lindenwood College, Mo.	The Family	Home Economics Department	6
Mount Union College, Ohio	The Family	Economics Department	11
Russell Sage College, N. Y.	Art and Science of Homemaking	Dean	12
State University of Iowa, Iowa	Modern Marriage	Department of Religion	13
Teachers College Columbia University	Family Social Relations	Interdepartmental	9

In 1937 Popenoe summarized the situation as follows: "The colleges are moving toward education for marriage . . . but they still have a long journey ahead of them. Of the courses in the family that are now available, too many are timid and pedantic, dealing with historical speculation about the primitive matriarchate, for instance, which will not arouse much anxiety in the minds of trustees or alumni and terminating safely in the colonial period or with a glance at the Industrial Revolution. The hearty welcome given to some really good courses now being taught is evidence that they will eventually become universal." [23 : 739]

Certainly the number of courses dealing with marriage and the family has multiplied rapidly since 1930. Approximately 50 colleges [29] offered courses in this field at the beginning of the decade, as contrasted with more than 450 colleges in 1940. "Professor Groves estimates that in 1938–39 such courses were given in 275 colleges and universities, an increase of 61 institutions over the previous academic year." [15 : 123] Many colleges now offer more than one course. An analysis of the 1940–41 catalogues of 508 accredited colleges and universities shows that 438 colleges offered 614 courses dealing with marriage and family living. Sociology departments continued to sponsor three-fourths of all courses listed, while home economics departments accounted for another 20 per cent. The increasing emphasis on preparation for marriage is also apparent in course titles and descriptions. Although catalogue information is known to lag far behind curriculum change, in 1940 one course title in five included the word marriage.

More detailed information about marriage courses is available through the National Association of Deans of Women. [5] Their list of 38 courses makes no pretense of being all-inclusive, yet gives reliable data on organization, methods, leadership, and emphasis which attempts to make a direct and vigorous approach to education for marriage.

Many marriage courses now perform a real service in at least partially filling the gap between theoretical instruction and youth's own practical problems of family adjustment. It is expected that if marriage courses really function in stimulating an awareness of potential contributions which the various subject matters can make to education for family living, "the faculty will be so sensitive to the needs of students in this area that study and discussion of family life will be pursued in all of the contexts to which it is pertinent." [31 : 530]

3:
The Problem and Method of Attack

COLLEGE faculty and administrators have become increasingly concerned that instruction in family problems shall develop in ways most significant to society and of greatest value to the student. Although still a relatively new field of instruction, the importance of education for marriage is being recognized.

The pioneer work of Groves [18] in focusing instruction on contemporary problems of the individual and family group led other teachers and community leaders to ask what really constitute the perplexing and vital problems of adjustment faced by family members today. Some instructors sought to determine the nature of such problems through interviews with social workers, psychologists, physicians, and professional associates. Others drew upon personal experience and the testimony of friends. Little help was available in the literature of sociology, home economics, and psychology. Research on the family dealt more often with the size and composition of the family, fecundity, age at marriage, and family law than with family interaction. Although textbooks continued to give much attention to social theory and little to personal relationships, Hart's survey of changing emphases in textbooks on the family, published between 1892 and 1932, indicates the beginning of a trend away from emphasis on primitive and historical aspects toward more consideration of psychological factors and personal social adjustments. [19]

Watson made a relatively new approach to the problem. He asked his class of nine students for recommendations on questions and problems vital to them, thus turning for suggestions to the consumer of instruction in marriage and the family. [27] The seven major areas of interest as indicated by frequency of questions were: preparation for parenthood, problems of sex before marriage, wise choice of mate,

19

husband-wife adjustment, birth control, divorce and unbroken family
life, and companionate marriage and other variations in form of marriage. Bell [6] and Butterfield [11] found personal interviews helpful
in discovering the anxieties of youth. Some other investigators [24],
however, question the value of the interview method in securing accurate information on more subtle, intangible, personal relationships.

Another device used to help the instructor become familiar with
the concerns of youth is the question box. To solicit suggestions at the
beginning of lectures or classes in marriage and family relations is not
an uncommon procedure. For instance, written questions asked by
more than 100 men and women registrants helped to determine both
content and method in an experimental course sponsored in 1937 by
several departments in a large urban university. [9] Leading in the
number of questions were these topics: choosing a mate, sex behavior
in marriage, conflict and adjustment in marriage, parenthood, the
family budget, the relation of the student to his parents, and romance
and realism in family married life. Revealing questions were collected from 333 boys and girls between the ages of 18 and 25 by
Butterfield [11] before and during informal group discussions. Their
"love problems" appeared to center around five general topics: starting
boy-girl relationships, making a good impression, keeping steady
company, engagement problems, and problems concerning marriage.

STATEMENT OF THE PROBLEM

The present study was undertaken to develop simple techniques
appropriate to mass exploration of the concerns and perplexities of
youth in the area of marriage and family living.

The problem was defined as follows: To ascertain what certain undergraduate students and alumni of two Pennsylvania colleges consider important material in instruction on marriage and the family,
and to suggest some implications of the findings in education for marriage and family living. Four basic assumptions were recognized:

1. Education for marriage and family life is both possible and desirable.

2 Young men and women have some understanding of what con-

stitutes for them important materials of instruction in family education.

3. Young men and women have fairly well-defined beliefs concerning the relative importance of materials of instruction in family education.

4. Young men and women will respond with sincerity, frankness,
and honesty to a request for suggestions and evaluation of materials of
instruction in family education.

DELIMITING THE PROBLEM

Two accredited institutions of higher education located in Pennsylvania, hereafter referred to as "S" and "T," were selected for study.
They were two among the 25 largest institutions of collegiate rank in
the United States in 1936. These colleges were chosen because both
were: (1) institutions with well-established schools of liberal arts, (2)
coeducational, (3) accessible, (4) known to the investigator, and (5)
willing and able to provide the desired number and type of participants needed. *The Educational Directory, 1936*, Part III, *Colleges and
Universities* * listed both institutions as accredited by the Middle States
Association of Colleges and Secondary Schools.

The total enrollment in the undergraduate schools at "S" in 1936–37
was 5,218, 1,482 of whom were full-time students enrolled in the School
of Liberal Arts. The total enrollment in the undergraduate schools at
"T" in 1936–37 was 6,287, of which number 851 were full-time students
enrolled in the School of Liberal Arts. Both "S" and "T" received public funds appropriated by the legislature of the State of Pennsylvania.
Eighteen per cent of the undergraduate students at "S" and 39 per cent
of the undergraduate students at "T" were women. In 1936–37 approximately 90 per cent of all undergraduate students at "S" and 83 per cent
of all undergraduate students at "T" officially registered as having a
home address in Pennsylvania.

"S" college is located in a rural district in the center of the state. The
resident population of the college town is listed as 6,226 in the 1940
census. Most of the students at "S" live in dormitories, fraternity
houses, or boarding houses in the town. In 1936–37 college dormitories

* Published by the Office of Education, United States Department of the Interior
(now the Federal Security Agency).

housed only 820 women and 288 men students. Houses maintained by fraternities accommodated approximately 1,450 men and 80 women in 1936–37, while 60 women lived in cooperative houses. College fees for the academic year, exclusive of room, board, and laboratory fees, amounted to $133.50 at "S." Room and board cost $300 to $380 per year. According to the Dean of Women, approximately 20 per cent of the women students earned part or all of their expenses. No estimate was available for men students, although many work in homes, fraternity houses, and college dining commons.

"T" college is located in a distinctly urban community with a population close to two million. Seventy-one per cent of all "T" undergraduate students with home addresses in Pennsylvania live in the city in which "T" is located. In 1936–37 college dormitories at "T" housed 150 women students. The college maintained no dormitories for men. Fraternity and sorority houses accommodated approximately 75 men and 65 women in 1936–37. There were no cooperative houses at "T" at that time. College fees at "T" for the academic year, exclusive of room, board, and laboratory fees, were $292. It is estimated by the personnel deans that about 65 per cent of all students were earning part or all of their college expenses.

Undergraduate students, classified as freshmen and seniors by the registrars of the institutions, and alumni who had received a bachelor's degree not less than one year nor more than five years prior to the investigation were selected as subjects for the present study. It was assumed that the college, family, and total experiences of freshmen, seniors, and recently graduated alumni were sufficiently different to warrant consideration of these three groups as separate units. Both men and women were included in the study. The majority of undergraduate students and all of the alumni participating in the study were selected from the schools of liberal arts.

Neither "S" nor "T" offered instruction in marriage or family relations other than advanced sociology courses dealing with the family as a social institution. These courses served a relatively small group of juniors and seniors majoring in sociology. Although the 1936–37 catalogue of "T" listed an additional course in family relations for prospective teachers of young children, students from the School of Liberal Arts could not elect this course. Therefore very few freshmen, seniors, and alumni at either "S" or "T" received classroom instruction in marriage and family relations prior to May, 1937. Only 79 freshmen and 34 seniors registered in schools other than liberal arts were used as subjects, and none of these students was majoring in home economics or parent education.

THE DEVELOPMENT OF TECHNIQUES

Techniques appropriate to the problem were developed and selected to fulfill, as completely as possible, the following purposes: (*a*) to establish and sustain rapport with individuals asked to participate in the investigation; (*b*) to stimulate free, frank, and discriminating response; (*c*) to ensure anonymity of the participants; (*d*) to minimize the operation of bias; (*e*) to reduce the number and influence of variables; and (*f*) to facilitate administration through the usual college organization.

TABLE I. *Student Groups Participating in Exploration of Given Techniques*

STUDENT GROUP PARTICIPATING	No. of PERSONS IN GROUP	TECHNIQUES EXPLORED				
		Inter-view	Written Response to:			
			Group Discussion	Inquiry Forms	Check Lists	Personal Data Forms
"R" freshmen..............	53	x	x	x	x	x
"R" sophomores and juniors.............	61	x	x	x	x	x
"S" juniors and seniors....	68		x	x	x	x
"T" juniors and seniors....	54	x	x	x	x	x
"T" alumni...............	32			x	x	x

Instruments and procedures appropriate to the problem were developed and subjected to trial and modification. Groups of undergraduates and alumni at "S" and "T" colleges and at a third college designated as "R" assisted in the exploration of techniques. Table I shows the number of persons and college class for each group. Individuals at "S" and "T" colleges who assisted in the exploratory period were not asked to participate later in the study. Techniques and procedures explored include informal and scheduled personal interviews, group discussion, and several methods of administering the inquiry forms, check lists, and data blanks.

For the trial interviews individual students were engaged in friendly conversation and asked for suggestions of what to include in an outline for functional instruction in marriage and family relations. This method was found to be time-consuming and difficult to control. Reserve concerning the more personal aspects of sex, conflict with parents, and dissatisfaction with present family life was noted. Some of the sociological data needed were difficult to obtain and to record accurately after the interview. Since the interview method failed to fulfill the accepted purposes, it was rejected as inappropriate for this study.

Informal discussions were held with two small social groups at "T" and an organized discussion group at "R" college. Questions were raised for discussion concerning material to include in preparing an outline for functional instruction in marriage and family relations. The secretary of each group and the investigator took notes on questions and suggestions. The bias of a dominant individual or vocal minority markedly influenced trends and values in group discussion. Several members of each group did not participate. Others contributed little to the group discussion but spoke freely in personal conferences after the meeting. Even stenographic notes did not report the periods of most active discussion. The group discussion method was therefore rejected as unsuitable for the study.

The free response inquiry forms were developed and tried with groups of students at "R" and "T" colleges. Each form consisted of a single page with two paragraphs typed at the top of the page. The heading "Will You Help" and the first paragraph telling of the development of instruction in marriage and family relations in other colleges were the same on each form. The second paragraph differed on the two forms. Form A_1* asked for specific suggestions concerning what the student would like to have discussed. Form B_1* asked for suggestions to be made in the light of the student's knowledge of the needs and interests of other classmates.

The investigator distributed alternate forms to students meeting in a regularly scheduled class period. Anonymous responses were re-

* See Appendix, Part III, page 178.

quested. No explanation other than a request for voluntary cooperation was given. At the end of 20 minutes, the investigator collected the papers, and then opened discussion about the effectiveness of this technique in securing free, frank, and discriminating response. The groups suggested minor changes in wording, recommended alternate seating to provide a greater degree of privacy, and discussed the possible value of a check list.

An average of 4.5 suggestions per student or a total of 258 separate items were received from the 57 students who used form A_1. Form B_1, which dealt with the needs of other students, received only 214 suggestions from 57 students or an average of 3.8 items per person. The suggestions given on Form B_1 were more often expressed in general than specific terms.

The advisers of the students at "R" and "T" analyzed the responses written during the regular class period. As far as they could tell, there was no evidence of jest or deliberate effort to conceal or deceive. Immediate personal problems were evident in many of the questions and suggestions.

Form A_1* was further revised and tried with a cooperating group in "S" college, using procedures identical to those at "T" college. This revised form secured free, frank, and discriminating responses from the group at "S" college, as evaluated by the instructors of the groups, two advisers, and the investigator. The procedure of administering the form made provision for establishing rapport and for reducing the operation of bias and variables. The form was relatively easy to administer through the usual college organization and facilities. The use of the free response inquiry form in regularly scheduled classes with the approval of the instructor and voluntary cooperation of students was therefore accepted as a satisfactory technique appropriate to the problem.

A check list consisting of a number of items which may not have been considered in the brief period permitted for free response was submitted to the test groups. The list was designed to secure an evaluation of items in certain aspects of marriage and family life. Thirty different topics, frequently mentioned in the free responses and believed to be representative, were listed in random order. Each topic had

* See Appendix, page 178.

to be rated on two different scales entitled respectively, "Value to Most Students" and "Value to You Personally." This check list, C_1, was presented to the cooperating groups at "R" college six weeks after their initial free response. Unlimited time was given for the rating of topics. The distribution of ratings on the scale "Value to You Personally" was wider than that on "Value to Most Students." A revision of the check list, using the five-point scale "Value to You Personally," was made to include specific questions instead of general topics. This form, C_2, was found adequate in terms of the purposes defined and was adopted as an instrument appropriate to the problem.

A personal data form was developed to secure sociological data which might have some association with responses. This form was tried with student groups at "R" college, revised, used with groups at "T" college, and revised again.* After satisfactory use with cooperating groups at "S" college the form was adopted.

PROCEDURES WITH UNDERGRADUATE STUDENTS AND ALUMNI

The final revisions of the various forms were presented to a group of freshmen at "T" to check procedures and timing. The instructor announced that regular class work for the day would be waived in favor of a special project in which several Pennsylvania colleges were participating. He said the study dealt with a new field of instruction in which student suggestions and reactions were needed, but he did not disclose its exact nature. The cooperation of the class members was requested but was not made mandatory, and the instructor left the room.

The investigator explained that student responses to three forms were needed, and that a code number instead of the student's name should be placed on each form. Time allocation was stated and anonymity assured. Student assistants distributed, in random order, cards bearing code numbers. Students were requested to take alternate seats in the classroom. The investigator then distributed the free response forms. At the end of 20 minutes all students were asked to stop writing, to fold the page once, and to pass it to the investigator. The check

---

* See final form in Appendix, page 183.

list was then distributed with a reminder to write in the code number. No further explanation was made. Unlimited time was permitted for checking. The student exchanged the check list for a personal data blank. The student returned this completed form to the investigator, who asked him to destroy his code card, and thanked and dismissed him. A few students completed the three forms in 35 minutes. All completed the assignment without pressure in the 50-minute class period. The group was quiet, cooperative, and intent on its work. Several students expressed sincere interest in the project and offered to assist further if needed. Since this procedure appeared to be satisfactory, it was adopted for further use.

The free response inquiry form * used with undergraduate students was modified to solicit more effectively the responses of alumni. It was mailed to 10 alumni of "T" college known to the investigator and to 10 who were not known. A personal letter asking for cooperation and a stamped, addressed return envelope were enclosed. Within two weeks answers were received from seven of the alumni known to the investigator and from three alumni not known. The responses appeared to be sincere, frank, and discriminating expressions of their opinions.

A revised procedure was then tested which used 12 alumni known to a popular member of "T" faculty. The alumni inquiry form, alumni code card, a stamped, addressed return envelope, and a personal letter from the staff member were mailed under one cover. A follow-up post card, P_1, signed by the staff member requesting cooperation was mailed one week later. Two weeks after the receipt of the return post card the check list and personal data form were mailed. These were followed, at intervals of two weeks, by a second post card, P_2, a third post card, P_3, and a supplementary information form. Complete responses were received from five of the 12 alumni and incomplete responses from four. The procedure seemed to establish rapport and to be relatively easy to administer. Although the technique provided little control of bias, variables, and selective factors operating in the population, it was accepted as feasible and sufficiently satisfactory to warrant use in the study.

* See Appendix, page 180.

THE POPULATION

As stated previously, participants in the study included freshmen and senior students and alumni from "T" and "S" colleges. In order to minimize bias associated with immediate interest and experience, students registered in sociology courses dealing primarily with the family were excluded from the group. Undergraduates and alumni from the respective Schools of Education were eliminated because of possible professional interest in units of instruction dealing with family life, parent education, or home and school relations. It was assumed that a population drawn largely from the Schools of Liberal Arts would base judgments and recommendations upon personal rather than professional experience, interest, and needs.

In each college certain sections of English composition, a required subject at both "T" and "S," were scheduled primarily for students in the School of Liberal Arts. These sections participated in the study. Since "T" and "S" required few specific courses of seniors, instructors of popular courses in history, government, Greek literature, English literature, drama, chemistry, and botany were asked to cooperate. Those sections were used in the study in which (1) a majority of the students were freshmen or seniors in the School of Liberal Arts, and (2) the instructor was generally well liked by students. The class roll was accepted as evidence of the predominance of liberal arts students. Faculty members known to have the confidence of undergraduates were asked to suggest the names of instructors and advisers well liked by students and believed to be sympathetic to instruction in marriage and family life. Some of the persons suggested were then asked to help in securing responses from both undergraduates and alumni. The Dean of the School of Liberal Arts, the professor in charge of the department, and cooperating instructors approved the project before classes were used.

All alumni receiving bachelor's degrees from the Schools of Liberal Arts at "T" and "S" colleges in the classes of 1932 to 1936 inclusive, for whom the alumni office could provide a correct address, were approached in the study. Cooperating advisers and instructors signed the personal letter addressed to those alumni whom they recalled. Advisers and instructors who participated in this section of the study included personnel deans, religious advisers, and instructors of English, German, Greek, botany, chemistry, geology, physical education, psychology, and sociology. A letter * signed by a well-known staff member at each institution solicited the cooperation of alumni not remembered.

TABLE 2. *Number of Participants Associated with Given Schools, Classified According to College, School, Class, and Sex*

COLLEGE, CLASS, AND SEX	NUMBER OF PARTICIPANTS ASSOCIATED WITH GIVEN SCHOOL †					ALL SCHOOLS
	Liberal Arts	Com-merce	Agri-culture	Engi-neering	Mineral Industries	
"T" freshman men.....	66	11				77
"T" freshman women..	10	9				19
"S" freshman men.....	110		21	19	19	170
"S" freshman women..	54					54
All freshmen........	241	20	21	19	19	320
"T" senior men.......	49	2				51
"T" senior women....	20	8				28
"S" senior men........	28		21	3		52
"S" senior women.....	33					33
All seniors..........	130	10	21	3		164
"T" alumni...........	29					29
"T" alumnae........	21					21
"S" alumni..........	65					65
"S" alumnae........	33					33
All alumni..........	148					148
All participants.......	519	30	42	22	19	632

† "S" college has no School of Commerce. "T" college has no School of Agriculture, Engineering, or Mineral Industries.

A total of 632 persons participated in the study. Of this group 225 (36 per cent) were affiliated with "T" and 407 (64 per cent) were affiliated with "S" college. Table 2 shows the distribution of participants by sex, college, class in college, and school affiliation. Approximately one half (320 or 51 per cent) of all participants were classified as freshmen, while the remainder was divided between seniors (26 per cent) and

* See Appendix, pages 179–180.

alumni (23 per cent). All the alumni in each institution had been affiliated with the School of Liberal Arts. A total of 371 undergraduates or 77 per cent of all freshmen and seniors included in the study were enrolled in the School of Liberal Arts. The groups of freshmen, seniors, and alumni from each institution included both men and women. Four hundred and forty persons, or 70 per cent of all participants, were men, and 188, or 30 per cent, were women.

Groups from "T" and "S" colleges differed significantly in distribution of location of present home, place of abode, religious affiliation, and estimated family income.* More than half of the "S" subjects came from homes located in towns and small cities, lived in dormitories, fraternity, or sorority houses, were Protestant, and reported a family income over $3,000 for the year preceding the collection of data. A majority of "T" subjects came from homes located in a very large city, lived with their families, were Jewish, and reported a family income less than $3,000 for the year preceding the collection of data. "S" seniors and alumni were very similar to "T" seniors and alumni, respectively, in mean chronological age and the amount of schooling completed by each parent. As a group "S" freshmen were older than "T" freshmen and their fathers and mothers had had more education than the parents of "T" freshmen. Groups from "T" and "S" were much alike with respect to their marital status, occupation of father, and mother, frequency of separation and divorce among parents, and degree of satisfaction with their present family life.

As could be expected, the classes differed significantly in chronological age and marital status. Freshmen were younger than seniors and fewer were married or engaged to be married. Alumni were older than seniors and many more alumni than seniors were married. In contrast to the undergraduate students alumni more frequently lived with their relatives and more frequently rated present family life as less than satisfactory.

The men participating in the study differed little from the women with respect to chronological age, location of present home, estimated family income, frequency of separation and divorce among parents, and ratings assigned present family life. More men than women were boarding. A larger proportion of fathers of women than of fathers of

* See Appendix, Part I, for data and statistics describing the population in detail.

men had completed college. At "S" a larger proportion of women than of men had fathers who were engaged in professional services. More significant differences were apparent between classes than between men and women or between groups from the two colleges. A more detailed analysis of population traits appears in the Appendix on pages 161–173.

ORGANIZATION OF DATA

Categories for the classification of data secured on free response forms and check lists were established as a result of group deliberation by an advisory committee of two men and two women. The committee included a professor of sociology, a dean of women, an instructor of parent education, and a Christian Association adviser. One hundred and fifty items, drawn at random from the free response forms and transferred to individual cards, were presented to the advisory committee to be classified in not less than seven or more than 12 categories. Each member devised his own groups based on the assumption that categories should (1) be appropriate to the data, (2) implement effective analysis of the data, (3) be descriptive, and (4) discriminate with a minimum of overlapping. The proposals of each member of the committee were pooled and a composite list of 10 categories was prepared. These were returned to the committee to be tested for adequacy through the independent classification of a second group of 150 randomly selected responses and of the 28 items on the check list.

The following categories were deemed to be satisfactory and were adopted for use in the analysis of data:

  I. The Family as a Social Institution
  II. Two and Three Generation Adjustments
  III. Premarriage Problems
  IV. Sex
  V. Accord in Family Adjustment
  VI. Discord in Family Adjustment
  VII. Family Economics
VIII. Children
  IX. Religion and Ethics
  X. Miscellaneous

An outline * was prepared to define the scope of each category and facilitate classification of individual responses.

Each item written on the free response forms was transcribed to a card and marked with the code number of the person who suggested it. The cards were classified under the 10 categories by the investigator and an assistant, each working independently. For a duplicate sample of 454 cards differences in classification occurred with only six cards.

Master sheets were prepared for recording the number of free response items suggested by each participant in each category, the data given on the Personal Data blanks, and the rating assigned to each item on the check lists. Data from the original forms were recorded on the master sheets and checked for accuracy of transcription. The data were summarized, organized to form tables, and subjected to statistical analysis.

TECHNIQUES FOR STATISTICAL ANALYSIS

The mean (M), percentage (P), and standard deviation (s), were selected to facilitate the description of participating groups. Other techniques were applied to test hypotheses relevant to the study and to generalize findings to a population larger than that actually observed. They included methods for testing the reliability of a difference between two means and between two percentages, the Chi-Square Test of the significance of differences, and analysis of variance.

The particular formula used in this study for the computation of the standard deviation of the difference between means was as follows:

$$s_{M1-M2} = \frac{N_1 s_1^2 + N_2 s_2^2}{N_1 + N_2 - 2} \cdot \frac{N_1 + N_2}{N_1 N_2}$$

The levels of significance accepted in interpreting the results of statistical analysis represented approximately an equal degree of probability. The critical region appropriate to this problem was defined by a deviation equal to that which would occur approximately once in one hundred times in random sampling. In terms of the ratio of the difference between two means or between two percentages to the standard deviation of the differences, 2.6 was considered the critical point. A

---

* This outline appears on pages 174–177 in the Appendix.

quotient greater than 2 and less than 2.6 was considered of questionable significance.

The critical point in computations using the Chi-square Test was defined as $\chi^2_{.01}$. Where a chi-square as large as or larger than $\chi^2_{.01}$ was obtained, the null hypothesis was rejected because it was not reasonable to maintain that the differences might have been produced by the fluctuations of random sampling alone. An observed chi-square with a probability between .05 and .01 was considered of questionable significance.

In analysis of variance problems the ratio of the interclass to the intraclass mean square, or the obtained F, was compared with $F_{.01}$ in Snedecor's tables [24 a]. Where the obtained F was as large as or larger than the table values for $F_{.01}$ for the corresponding number of degrees of freedom, it was understood that the probability of variation of that size resulting from sampling accidents alone was less than one chance in one hundred. Where the observed F was smaller than the F to be expected at the 5 per cent level of significance ($F_{.05}$) the null hypothesis was maintained. An observed F between $F_{.05}$ and $F_{.01}$ was considered to be of questionable significance.

The selection of the participants was designed to secure as representative a sample of "T" and "S" freshman, senior, and alumnus suggestions and evaluations as was feasible within the limits of this study. The characteristics which determined the selection of participation at "T" and "S" were: official classifications as freshman, senior, or alumnus in the classes of 1932 to 1936 inclusive; enrollment in or graduation from a curriculum involving little or no consideration of problems of marriage and family life; and enrollment in the alumni records as graduates from the School of Liberal Arts or in classes designed to meet the needs of freshman and senior liberal arts students.

No effort was made to secure proportionate representation of each class, sex, or college. Several factors undoubtedly limit the representativeness of the sample. For instance, while the selection of classes in English composition designed to serve freshmen enrolled in the School of Liberal Arts made it possible to reach a relatively large number of these students, it reduced the chances of participation of students with irregular schedules. It is probable that the suggestions and evaluations of freshmen who had schedules rendered irregular by the need of free hours for employment, athletic participation, unusual activities, or health care, are not represented adequately in this study. The use of classes in areas of selected subject matter open to seniors in the School of Liberal Arts probably limited the participation of upperclassmen with certain professional goals. Prospective physicians, lawyers, and accountants had to register in a number of pre-professional classes not used by the investigator. This reduced their chance of contributing suggestions and evaluations. Alumni representation was limited by the fact that contact could be made only with those alumni for whom correct names and addresses were available. Although there is no way of knowing how closely the sample of suggestions and evaluations in this study resembles the whole range and variety of freshman, senior, and alumnus suggestions and evaluations, the great preponderance of similarity over difference within various sub-groups suggests that a fairly adequate sampling was obtained.

No claim is made that the observed population of this study is a random sample of any existent population. The undergraduates participating in the study do not constitute a random sample of freshmen or of seniors, of "T" undergraduates or of "S" undergraduates, of college men or of college women. The two essential assumptions underlying claims to random sampling from any existent population were violated because every member of any given group of undergraduates or alumni did not have equal opportunity to be chosen and the choice of each participant was not unprejudiced by the choice of any other participant. The participants observed in this study were the result of purposive selection. There is no way of determining the reliability of the likenesses and differences observed or in what ways this sample truly represents the real population from which it was drawn. Generalizations, therefore, were made to a hypothetical population. The findings of the several tests of significance do not apply to all "S" and "T" students and alumni or to older youth. They relate to the unknown hypothetical population of which the group participating in this study is assumed to be a random sample.

4:
Suggestions Concerning Materials of Instruction On Marriage and Family Life

THE written questions or suggestions expressing what each participant believed should be included in college instruction designed to help young men and women make more satisfying adjustments in relation to marriage and family life varied widely in number and type. The volume of the total response per person ranged from one brief sentence of six words to several pages including more than 800 words. Each separate question or suggestion is hereafter called an item. Eighty-three persons or 13 per cent of the total group suggested only one item, but frequently the one suggestion was elaborated in considerable detail. More than half of the participants (369 persons or 58.4 per cent of the total group) suggested from two to five items. Approximately one-fourth of the total group participating in the study suggested at least six and not more than 10 items, while only 16 persons, or 2.6 per cent of all participants, suggested more than 10 items. The mean number of items per person was 4.4. Since the time available for writing on the free response form was limited to the first 20 minutes of a regularly scheduled class or conference period, a response including many items necessarily treated each briefly. Control of the amount of time used by alumni for writing responses was not attempted. Although alumni presumably had more time for response, they tended to suggest fewer items than undergraduate students. The distribution of free response items among groups of participants is summarized in Table 3.

The response of individual participants varied not only in number of items but in the areas of marriage and family life discussed. Where

TABLE 3. *Number of Items Pertaining to Instruction in Marriage and Family Life, Suggested by 632 Participants, Classified According to College, Class, and Sex*

COLLEGE, CLASS, AND SEX	NUMBER OF PERSONS	ITEMS SUGGESTED BY GIVEN GROUPS OF PARTICIPANTS	
		Total	Mean
"T" freshman men	77	284	3.7
"T" freshman women	19	78	4.1
"S" freshman men	170	677	4.0
"S" freshman women	54	251	4.6
All freshmen	320	1,290	4.0
"T" senior men	51	232	4.6
"T" senior women	28	177	6.3
"S" senior men	52	296	5.7
"S" senior women	33	186	5.6
All seniors	164	891	5.4
"T" alumni	29	95	3.3
"T" alumnae	21	83	4.0
"S" alumni	65	244	3.8
"S" alumnae	33	149	4.5
All alumni	148	571	3.9
All "T" participants	225	964	4.3
All "S" participants	407	1,788	4.4
All men	444	1,828	4.1
All women	188	924	4.9
All participants	632	2,752	4.4

more than one question or suggestion was given the items frequently were distributed among several categories. The total responses of two participants suggesting items in several areas illustrate the scope of items suggested by a single person.*

Participant 864721, an alumnus of "S," was 24 years old, married, lived in an apartment with his wife, rated his family life ideal, and estimated the annual income between $1,500 and $3,000 per year.

* The Roman numeral to the left of each item indicates the category in which it was classified.

IV.   I feel that in college students should be given good frank instruction on sex, and I am not sure that the present course is adequate. I should say in my case experience was the teacher, not college.

III.   Too many enter marriage hurriedly. It should be pointed out that it is important before considering marriage to consider similarity of interests and general compatibility other than the bliss of new romance.

V.   I feel too that, on either the part of the prospective husband or wife, there should be some grasp of current problems and some appreciation of literature and fine arts, as a home without some of this would appear to me quite barren. There should also be some discussion somewhere of the responsibilities of marriage.

V.   Finally it should be emphasized somewhere to the young people that marriage and home life are a proposition which require that both the man and the woman go 75% of the way. They should realize that patience, broadmindedness, and tolerance are required if little misunderstandings are not to wreck marital happiness.

Participant E40, a senior woman at "T," was 21 years old, single, lived in a sorority house, rated her present family life ideal, and estimated the family income to be over $10,000 per year.

VII.   What is the least amount of money a family of five can live on? What is the least amount of money one may marry on?

IV.   A complete discussion of sex including coitus, birth control, knowledge of social disease, etc.

VII.   Is there any real harm in the wife's working at the onset of marriage?

III.   What should be the relation between the ages of husband and wife?

VII.   Does it make for a happy family life if the standard of living is lowered from the one accustomed to when single?

IV.   Would marriage be more successful if taboos on sex were lifted during the engagement period?

IV.   How can one adjust oneself without embarrassment at the beginning of marriage to living with one of the opposite sex?

VII.   What arrangements should be made for allowances and budgets? Who should handle it?

V.   How can one still keep all the friends and associations, such as club membership, after marriage and still have a happy home?

IX.   Is it wise to marry out of one's religion?

V.   What is the value (besides pleasant memories) of weddings and honeymoons? Are there any disadvantages?

V.   Should one always tell the truth to one's mate or is it better to keep things hidden because at the moment they may cause an argument?

It was evident in many responses that the written questions and suggestions reflected some of the immediate personal problems of the subject. No attempt was made, however, to analyze individual cases where the association of personal data and total free response was quite apparent. The total response of three subjects who appeared to reveal personal problems on the free response form are quoted.

Participant E160, a freshman woman at "T," was 19 years old, single, lived at home, rated her family life unsuccessful, and gave no estimate of family income.

Who is the "man" in the family?

Should parents plan their children's life for them and expect them to carry it out?

Should the children be expected to follow in their parents' footsteps as far as a career is concerned?

Should financial matters rule family discord?

What can be done to help broaden the minds of some parents concerning their children's future?

How can parents draw their children closer to them instead of driving them away?

Are parents to be rulers or companions?

Participant E36, a senior at "T," was 20 years old, engaged to be married, lived at home, rated his family life satisfactory, and estimated the family income between $3,000 and $5,000.

Since I am engaged to be married, I would not be particularly interested in discussions of methods of contacting members of the opposite sex, or of finding a most suitable mate. I have already done that. My problems are now those of ignorance as to best means of social, mental, and physical harmony; I would appreciate instruction as to the following:

Finding and emphasizing common mental interests and objectives, also common recreational interests so as to grow closer socially and mentally.

Some idea of the underlying ideals of and reasons for marriage as a social and ethical institution. I wish to know and appreciate these ideals.

Specific remedies and cures for the frequent minor differences as to the daily conduct of the married career—if these can be eliminated, i.e., the prevention of minor quarrels.

Sex information, e.g., birth control adequately explained.

Explanation of the sexual act as an art in itself, which it should be. Physical requirements such as health in general, freedom from defects, etc., necessary to be fulfilled for a successful physical side of marriage.

Consideration of differences between male and female psychology.

Participant 712358, an alumnus of "S," was 29 years old, engaged to be married, lived at home, rated his family life indifferent, and estimated the family income between $5,000 and $10,000. Neither parent had gone beyond the eighth grade in school.

Any attempt to list the problems of college students as they meet them when they have left school would be an almost inexhaustible jumble of differences not often recognized as problems. In other words, the nature of the problem must first be recognized. At any rate, here are some of the things that might be considered by an undergraduate for his future happiness:

1. The ability to recognize a problem of adjustment from a definite break in relationships.

2. What may happen to college graduates when they return to an old mode of living that is repulsive to them, but to which they must be subjugated for uncontrollable reasons. How is this to be met?

3. In terms of economic standards, what can college educated people (middle-class colleges) be happy with; whether it be in the city or country?

4. Some attempt should be made to determine the extent of obligation to one's parents. How far should this go? Even if the parents' situation seems precarious, but not in immediate danger, should the ex-college student spoil his chance of future happiness in order to repay the obligation?

5. The student should learn the most painless way to try his "wings," so that he can show that he is no longer the family child, but desires to live his own life. Naturally various cases must be considered here.

6. The problem of educated children of parents who have not had that opportunity should be considered at great length. The lack of adjustment and misunderstanding here is often of fatal consequences for any future relationships.

At each institution student advisers whose names were frequently mentioned as those to whom students would turn for guidance in personal problems of marriage and family life believed the responses were both frank and representative. There was no evidence of deliberate effort to conceal or distort.

Most of the items suggested for discussion by freshmen, seniors, and alumni concerned topics of interest to all, regardless of college class. In some instances the similarity of reaction and method of expression were so marked that identification by group, i.e., freshmen, seniors, alumni, without reference to the code number was almost impossible. In other cases the phraseology or manner of approach to a topic varied considerably from group to group, although the underlying thought appeared to be similar. Freshmen were unlikely to state their problems in terms of personal issues: "How to convince my parents that I should be allowed to do at home the same things I do in college, such as staying out late, etc." Seniors more often expressed themselves in general terms: "The adjustment of children (especially from 15 to 25 years of age) to their home environment." Among alumni comments on matters pertaining to the family and the individual there seemed to be more maturity of thought, not only in method of expression but also in grasp of the situation: "The problem of educated children of parents who have not had that opportunity should be considered at great length. The lack of adjustment and misunderstanding here is often of fatal consequences for any future relationships." Although the three suggestions deal with the same general problem, they are stated in different terms.

ILLUSTRATIONS OF TYPES OF SUGGESTIONS RECEIVED AND OF THEIR CLASSIFICATION IN CATEGORIES

I. THE FAMILY AS A SOCIAL INSTITUTION

Suggestions dealing with the family as a social institution were classified under the headings: (A) Origin and History of Marriage and the Family, (B) The Family in Society Today, and (C) The Future of the Family. On these topics only 10 freshmen, 18 seniors, and 12 alumni suggested items. It may be recalled that 29 freshmen, 131 seniors, and 112 alumni reported that they had taken at least one college course in sociology. The responses dealing with the family as a social institution were few in number and scattered in emphasis. Comments of freshmen, seniors, and alumni indicated a wide variety of interests and concerns.

A. Origin and History of Marriage and the Family

Only four persons gave suggestions dealing with the origin and history of marriage and the family. All the items suggested are listed to show their scope.

FRESHMAN
Has the purpose of marriage changed within the last one hundred years?

SENIOR
What is the ethnological development of marriage?

ALUMNI
College undergraduates, especially underclassmen, should be more impressed with the traditional and historical importance of the family relationship, and should be encouraged to inspect their own families with an eye to tracing definite traits, for the purpose of gaining tolerance toward other members of the family, and of concentrating for themselves the finest traits and traditions of the family. A family like a race can stand for something, often without realizing it. Thought may reveal what the family, as crystallized in the thinking descendant, might mean at its best.

A study of the history of the family as the unit of social structure will help. It will show why it has survived in spite of all its faults and criticisms.

B. The Family in Society Today

Suggestions concerning the family in society today fell into five subgroups: (1) the family as a primary or basic social institution, (2) function of marriage and the family, (3) relation of the family as an institution to the community, (4) social problems of the family as an institution, and (5) changing status of woman in society. On these topics four freshmen, 10 seniors, and seven alumni gave suggestions. Responses representative of the respective classes are quoted as illustrations under each sub-group.

1. The family as a primary or basic social institution

Little interest was apparent in topics dealing with the family as a social institution.

FRESHMEN
No comment.

SENIOR

Instruction setting forth the worthwhileness of the family and necessity for its maintenance should be given.

ALUMNUS

It strikes me that marriage is the most important contract in life. The integrity of the family depends on it and the structure of society has its foundation in the family. The speed of the divorce mill is an argument for the regulation of marriage.

2. *Function of marriage and the family*

The level of interest does not seem to be quite the same in the following comments but indirectly they may bear on the same subject.

FRESHMEN

No comment.

SENIORS

Is marriage necessary?

Some idea of the underlying ideals of and reasons for marriage as a social and ethical institution. I wish to know and appreciate these.

ALUMNI

No comment.

3. *Relation of the family as an institution to the community*

The response in this area from all three groups—freshman, senior, alumnus—was negligible.

FRESHMEN

No comment.

SENIOR

Place of the family in the community.

ALUMNUS

An understanding of the community, its part in the family and family's part in it is most important. This includes government, church and school.

4. *Social problems of the family as an institution*

Comments were received from only two alumni on this subject.

FRESHMEN

No comment.

SENIORS

No comment.

ALUMNI
Cultural values of family life. The home in the present civilization. What about our ideals today?

It should consist of the problems facing the modern family today—economic, social, and political problems.

5. Changing status of women in society

Both freshmen and seniors of only one institution ("T") were concerned with the changing status of women in society. This college is located in a large urban center where many women are employed outside the home.

FRESHMAN
Changing status of women in society is gradually changing conditions of marriage. This is of vital importance since women do not wish to be subordinate and take up family life as it should be.

SENIOR
Changed attitude toward position of women.

C. The Future of the Family

Suggestions concerning the future of the family fell into two subgroups: (1) probable future developments and (2) eugenics or race improvement. On these topics four freshmen, seven seniors, and three alumni commented.

1. Probable future developments

Only two questions appeared in this sub-group, one suggested by a freshman and one by a senior.

FRESHMAN
A study of the average American family would bring about desirable changes in many homes now and in the future.

SENIOR
What are the chances for economic security within the family in the future social order?

2. Eugenics or race improvement

On this subject a decided interest was shown by freshmen, seniors, and alumni. There was considerable repetition of questions to confirm the interest.

FRESHMAN
Should not the study of eugenics and heredity be placed in the curriculum of every college student?

SENIOR
It is desirable that people have some knowledge of genetics before choosing their mates so as to produce better children.

ALUMNUS
Eugenics: Include genetics—although it is pitifully underdeveloped.

II. TWO AND THREE GENERATION ADJUSTMENTS

This category implies a diversity of aims and standards converging under one roof, with certain evident points of strain. In some areas these points loom large, as indicated by the barrage of questions asked by freshmen, seniors, and alumni.

A. Parent-Student Adjustments

Problems of parent-student adjustment appeared to be vital, and in many cases teeming with conflict. Freshman suggestions frequently were colored by strong feeling. However, some senior and alumni comments indicated a highly emotionalized response. Suggestions dealing with parent-student adjustments fell into six sub-groups: (1) achieving independence, (2) confidences, affection between parent and student, (3) conflict of ideas and standards, (4) parental control of boy-girl relationships and behavior, (5) obligations of youth to parents, and (6) parent role in choice of vocation. On this subject 75 freshmen, 30 seniors, and 14 alumni expressed themselves.

Inasmuch as expressed concerns in parent-student adjustments varied in feeling tone among freshmen, seniors, and alumni, illustrations have been grouped to show variations.

1. Achieving independence

Freshman conflict appeared to be centered around an intense emotional struggle for freedom from parental control. Seniors, more independent by virtue of age, seemed to have lost some of the emotional intensity of freshmen and to have adopted a feeling of responsibility for achieving adjustment between their parents and themselves. Alumni appeared to have accepted parent-student adjustment as a basic issue and in several cases recommended strategy as a wise means to the goal of independence. There are alumni, however, whose mature reflections were colored with bitter realizations of personal struggles.

FRESHMEN

Up until what age should parents "lord" over their children? Or in other words, when is a boy or girl usually capable of choosing his own friends, hours and actions? Is it possible for parents to be too strict with their children in social life?

How much should your parents tell you what to do, and name specific examples with explanations where you should be on your own feet.

Should children do as parents say even though they know it to be stupid and wrong?

Just what is the extent of my independence of my parents? As a student of less than voting age, yet assumedly on an equal plane of intelligence with my parents, who have had less education, am I justified in making my own decisions as to habits and pursuits?

SENIORS

The right and freedom of the children and of the parents.

What are the chief reasons of maladjustment between parents and children?

The question of parental education and instruction of parents to see changing conditions of economics, sex, etc., with relation to their children.

The question of more freedom to think. Parents do not give children a chance to express themselves fearlessly without subjection to scolding or ridicule.

ALUMNI

The student should learn the most painless way to try his wings so that he can show that he is no longer the family child, but desires to live his own life. Naturally various cases must be considered.

Keeping respect, also cool head, and love for parents who always seem to be offering far-fetched and old-fashioned ideas.

I believe college men and women should be taught to think and act independently. In this respect the American colleges and the average American home fail miserably. The college graduate is too often unable to stand on his own. The young married man and woman should not be bound each to his own family. It is a shock to some who have been "tied to their mother's apron string" to learn for the first time that a child's worst handicap is his own parents and particularly his own mother. Yet it is important for them to realize this in their own lives and with respect to the children whom they themselves will probably rear.

2. *Confidence, affection between parent and student*

Relations of confidence, tolerance, and affection between parent and child, the opposite side of the picture of parent-student conflict, were topics of interest comparable to the issues of conflict. It may be that the existence of discord induced a yearning for accord and a questioning of the causes of maladjustment.

FRESHMEN

How can parents draw their children closer to them instead of driving them away?

My parents and I don't mix together as well as I should like us to. We have good times together but at the dinner table, for example, we do not joke and have as much fun as we should have. Each one of us sometimes thinks of his own problems and there is not enough cheerful and uplifting conversation although there is some. Perhaps this is because I am the only child.

What can be done to narrow the gap found between son or daughter and his or her own parents?

What relation exists between the student's parents in the way of happiness and family harmony? What type parents does he have, nagging or reassuring?

I believe one of the greatest problems of family life to be the temperament of the parents. This can make or break family life. If one of the parents is to become irritated by his or her work, or by some petty thing concerning only himself, if he has a bad temper he can spoil the family relations for many days at a time. My ideal in family life is one in which the mother and father are two pals with their children and do not treat them as if they were younger but as if they were old friends.

SENIORS

Questions such as those concerning confidences of personal things and asking advice of one's parents.

How may one be an understanding parent without being a moral preacher or an "old fogy"?

ALUMNI

How can two males live satisfactorily under one roof? What psychological adjustments must an unmarried son undergo in order to maintain a happy (1) father and son relationship, (2) mother and son relationship? To be sure, an adult son has neither a biologic nor economic right to hang around the hearthstone (invalids excepted). Circumstances, however, very often do not permit an early withdrawal.

By the time they reach college age probably most young people are rather "set" in their relationship as sons and daughters, brothers and sisters. However, it would not be too late to show them that parents are still a good thing to have and that just because they are about to step out on their own is no reason for them to neglect parents. Probably the sons' and daughters' and fathers' and mothers' angle could be interwoven, some of the ideas to be used in the present and some in the future.

3. *Conflict of ideas and standards*

One of the problems appearing as evidence of student concern is that of conflict of ideas and standards between parents and student. This concern, however, appears to be more definitely crystallized for the boy or girl in "T" college where the large majority of students live at home than in "S" where the parents of the great majority of students live in communities apart from the college. However, the alumnus whose comment is quoted below attended "S" college.

FRESHMEN

Are your parents alert and interested in all that surrounds them, or are they staid and settled and reluctant to change their ideas and mode of living?

A student is sometimes placed in embarrassing situations in his town because of actions of a parent. Should he "stick it out" in that town or move where he is not known?

SENIORS

To the student living at home the problem of acquainting an older generation with the thoughts and customs common to the new generation is a vital one. How to do it with the fewest possible hurts on both sides is a necessary part of a course in family relationships.

How can the parents be taught to understand the child's viewpoint? This matter of staying out late at night is a bone of contention in many families of college students as well as of high school students. The parents do not seem to understand that this is the twentieth century and things have changed since they were young.

ALUMNUS

What may happen to college graduates when they return to an old mode of living that is repulsive to them but to which they must be subjected for uncontrollable reasons? How is this to be met?

4. *Parental control of boy-girl relationships and behavior*

Both freshmen and seniors from the two colleges were concerned with problems of parental control of boy-girl relationships. Alumni did not appear to be interested in this aspect of the parent-student adjustments.

FRESHMEN

Should your parents choose your friends?

Have the parents a natural right to choose mates for their sons and daughters?

How much should one's family be considered when one thinks of getting married?

Should a parent intervene on a question of the marriage of a member of the family to the point where they will absolutely stop a prospective marriage?

SENIORS

The question of the family in relation to the friends outside the home is important. The problem of entertaining friends at home is one of no little importance.

What about marriage against the choice or wishes of the parents?

What is there for a girl to do if she is forced by her parents to marry a man that she does not love? How would it be possible for her to keep from doing this?

Should parents interfere between two people who wish to marry while in school?

ALUMNI

No comment.

5. *Obligations of youth to parents*

Out of the labyrinth of parent-student adjustments emerges the question of obligations of youth to parents, which, of course, is the problem of resistance to parental interference thrown into reverse. Factors, both psychological and economic, goad the student to reflections of duty.

Freshman and alumni interests parallel one another more nearly than do those of seniors with either group. For instance, freshmen and alumni both asked to what extent the individual is entitled to personal happiness at the expense of other members of the family. Freshmen wanted to know if they had the right to accept parental sacrifice for a college education. Alumni wanted to know, having accepted the college education, to what extent they were obligated to surrender opportunities for future success and happiness in order to repay any sacrifices parents might have made. No senior seemed exercised over either angle of this particular problem. On the other hand, seniors were troubled by the conflict in homes housing three generations. This latter problem challenged neither freshmen nor alumni.

FRESHMEN

Should any member of a family consider his own happiness in preference to the welfare, or at the expense of other members of his immediate family?

Just how much one's family means to a college student and the things he owes to that family.

When the child has reached the college age just what privileges can he expect to receive from the family, and in turn what duties is he responsible for?

I have very often been troubled by the question, "Am I depriving my family of many pleasures and necessities by going to college?" Perhaps this course could take problems similar to this into consideration.

Should parents deprive themselves of bare necessities to send their children to college?

SENIORS

How to prevent animosity between the two or three generations.

How successful are the lives of the members of families where there are three generations living in one house? What specific adjustments are necessary?

Difference in older generation's outlook on life and how to avoid excessive conflicts when outsiders are living together in the home.

How parents should prepare for the empty nest stage in their family life.

ALUMNI

Should the son or daughter get married if they are the sole means of support in the family, or should they give up the idea?

Some attempt should be made to determine the extent of obligation to one's parents. How far should this go? Even if the parents' situation seems precarious, but not in immediate danger, should the ex-college student spoil his chance of future happiness in order to repay that obligation?

6. Parent role in choice of vocation

The resistance of student to parental interference in the choice of career seemed to be a freshman problem.

FRESHMEN

Should the children be expected to follow in their parent's footsteps as far as a career is concerned?

Should parents plan their children's lives for them and expect them to carry it out?

How to get my parents to allow me to get in the right course, the one I want to take.

Should the parents be allowed to choose a vocation for their son or daughter?

B. Adjustments to Relatives after Marriage

Questions and comments concerning adjustments to relatives after marriage fell into two sub-groups: (1) when and how to live with the family after marriage, and (2) obligations to relatives. On this subject 21 freshmen, 22 seniors, and three alumni commented.

1. When and how to live with the family after marriage

The problem of after-marriage adjustments to relatives, the "in-law" problem, challenged the interest of freshmen, seniors, and alumni in both institutions. The points of emphases seem evenly distributed among all groups.

FRESHMEN

Ways to improve family relationships with the maternal and paternal relations.

How may a young couple successfully and without hard feelings break away from their respective parents-in-law? or would it be possible to get the laissez-faire idea across to the parents? Must we marry orphans?

SENIORS

If a member of the family of husband or wife is living with them, how should this be controlled to prevent friction in the family life?

Is it possible to legislate against a married couple living with relatives of either person?

ALUMNI

The inadvisability of a continued relationship with "in-laws."

I have learned through experience that the "in-law" problem cannot be minimized. If anything, it grows more acute with time and becomes more complicated after the grandchildren are born. I do not know if this can be taught in college but I think it would be well to stress that practically no problems which present themselves before marriage change for the better after marriage.

2. Obligations to relatives

The interrelationship of economic obligations of youth to parents and parents to youth was one of freshman-senior interest only.

FRESHMEN

Should a married man help support his parents?

Should "in-laws" depend on their children for financial aid?

Should a young married couple live with the husband's or wife's family for a short time until they get a start?

SENIORS

Children supporting parents . . . should they live together or maintain separate establishments?

What should be the relation between newly married couples and their parents, especially if the parents are financially dependent upon them?

What should a newly married couple do if the husband is unable to support them, yet both come from well-to-do homes and would be welcomed back?

ALUMNI

No comment.

III. PREMARRIAGE PROBLEMS *

Suggestions dealing with premarriage problems were classified under the headings: (A) Whom to Marry, (B) When to Marry, (C) Courtship Adjustments, and (D) Youth Relationships. On these subjects 316 freshmen, 164 seniors, and 36 alumni commented.

A. Whom to Marry

Freshmen and seniors suggested many more questions dealing with whom to marry than did alumni. This is reasonable, since relatively few undergraduate students were married or engaged. The questions of undergraduate students concerned concrete factors to be sought when choosing a mate, factors which would contribute to ultimate compatibility.

Suggestions and comments concerning the topic "Whom to Marry" centered around two somewhat generalized questions: (1) who should and should not marry, and (2) how to choose a mate. From these generalizations emerge a number of particularized questions dealing with specific factors to be considered in selecting a husband or wife. On the subject of whom to marry, 167 freshmen, 96 seniors, and 17 alumni commented.

1. Who should and should not marry

The question concerning "Who should and should not marry?" was asked repeatedly by freshmen and seniors but infrequently by alumni. When mentioned by alumni, however, the queries often suggested factors given no consideration by undergraduates. For instance, in the following illustrations, freshmen and seniors do not question the merits of marriage. Their problem is to choose wisely their mate. On the other hand, the alumni first balance the merits of single against married life before attempting their choice.

* See Sections IV and VII for premarital sex adjustments and finance problems.

FRESHMAN
The question of what type of person is usually able to carry on a successful marriage could be discussed.

SENIOR
What qualities should I look for which will bring companionship, mutual affection, and understanding?

ALUMNI
Trying to learn what marriage means—what a single life means—so that we can choose intelligently the one or the other.

Marriage, *per se,* should not be taught as the ultimate goal of each individual. Too often people are really not meant for marriage and do not only themselves but their family an injury by forcing their lives into that mold. Marriage should be based on many points of compatibility, physical, emotional, cultural, social, etc., all of which can be studied in college and a knowledge (though not a complete understanding) of them acquired.

2. *Choice of mate*

Questions dealing with how to choose a mate were asked repeatedly by freshmen and seniors, but infrequently by alumni. When asked by alumni, they were likely to indicate a crystallization of thought on the part of the questioner. Freshmen and seniors asked for specific information to help them make decisions. Alumni tended to point out conclusions born of reflection and experience.

FRESHMAN
How to choose a good wife. What qualities she should possess and what she should be capable of doing.

SENIOR
How to go about selecting a mate with whom you expect to spend the rest of your life?

ALUMNUS
The knowledge of how to select a living partner is necessary and may well be taught in college by teaching students to judge objectively their own qualities and those of others.

The following list of specific factors to be considered grew out of the more general question of how to choose a mate:

    a. Role of heredity, health, and physical qualifications.

    b. Role of education and intellectual level.

    c. Role of social status and background.

    d. Role of likes and dislikes, interests.

e. Role of personality.

f. Role of religion, race, and nationality.

g. Role of age differential.

h. Role of love.

i. Role of infatuation.

j. How to know if choice is right one.

For the most part questions on these topics were raised by freshmen and seniors rather than by alumni. Alumni interest appeared to center on compatibility as an integrated whole, while undergraduate interest was directed to diverse individual factors. Freshman and senior questions indicated great interest in the means to the end; alumni questions, in the end itself.

a. Role of heredity, health and physical qualifications. Freshmen revealed much the greater interest in the role of heredity, health, and physical qualifications. Given below are practically all the questions asked in this category. Freshmen asked twice as many questions as seniors. Alumni made no comment.

FRESHMEN

Instruction should be given to the two persons involved so that they will trace each other's family heredity before tying the bonds of marriage.

What types of men and women should or should not marry to produce most intelligent and healthiest families.

Personal health: should it be considered before people marry?

Health for both parties concerned should be stressed. Ill health of one party soon causes the other party to seek other interests and to pity instead of love.

Should a girl marry if she knows definitely she cannot have children?

If you know you have active T.B. and are in love, should you break the affair up?

Should a person marry when his family are all inclined to be tubercular?

SENIORS

A study of possibilities of marrying someone to improve the physical condition of your children over your own physical conditions.

What standards of health are required for marriage?

The choosing of a mate that is physically fit.

ALUMNI

No comment.

b. Role of education and intellectual level. The problem of the person with college training marrying a person without such training appeared to trouble undergraduates. Freshmen placed more emphasis upon this factor than seniors. Alumni made no direct comment.

FRESHMEN
Should the man and woman be equally well educated or should the man be superior in this respect?

Should a college graduate marry a person who is not a college graduate? Is this an advisable thing to do?

Are college love affairs usually successful?

If the woman is of superior intelligence, will that tend to an unhappy state?

SENIORS
What are the intellectual requirements for a happy marriage?

Should I as a person with culture and training marry a person who has little training?

What are the chances of a successful marriage where one partner is college-trained and the other is not?

ALUMNI
No comment.

Out of the depths of concern on this subject rises one battle cry from a freshman boy.

Make the college women more marriageable. We read that only a small percentage of them marry. A very unpleasant situation. I suppose personality and attitude to life is a great factor.

c. Role of social status and background. Closely allied to the role of education and intellectual level is that of social status and background. Comment is made only by freshmen and seniors. While the underlying thought of both groups appears to coincide, methods of expression reveal greater maturity on the part of seniors than of freshmen.

FRESHMEN
Should a person refrain from marriage because his would-be partner has a poor background?

Should a girl look for a man who has plenty of money and no background, or one she really loves? One can't be happy on love alone.

Should the background of one's wife be considered before marriage?

Is it well to marry above or below one's station in life?

Can two people with widely different cultural tastes ever "make a go" of marriage?

Should a couple marry when each one has lived under different economic conditions or in different social and spiritual fields?

SENIORS

Is it necessary for a successful marriage to have the partners in the marriage of similar cultural traits, backgrounds, and attitudes?

What are the social requirements for a happy marriage?

Correlation between the social and economic status of two people and its effect on their living successfully together.

What does one need culturally for a successful marriage?

What will our family backgrounds do toward helping or hindering our happiness?

How much should we know about the past family of the person we are contemplating marrying? How to go about finding this out?

ALUMNI

No comment.

d. Role of likes, dislikes, and interests. Freshmen asked the greater number of questions on the subject of likes and dislikes. All groups seemed to place the same value upon the advisability of choosing a mate with similar interests.

FRESHMEN

Primarily important in my estimation is choosing a husband or wife who has in general dislikes and likes similar to yours. In view of this, instruction in character study might be helpful.

Degree of similarity of interests of husband and wife necessary to ensure successful marriage.

Should a couple marry whose likes differ?

How much discrepancy in interests can exist between two parties to a marriage contract and yet have the experiment successful?

SENIORS

I believe a man must find a wife with common interests because it is inevitable that physical love cannot exist indefinitely. The pair must find happiness, contentment in doing things together, yet too much similarity of ideas will not be conducive to compatibility. The wife should be of fine ideals, characterized by sound common sense.

A person should be given help in studying his own make-up, thereby enabling him to judge what type of person would be suited for him. The interests of both parties should be alike on most lines.

Do we have the same aims in life? What should that aim tend toward?

ALUMNUS
Young men and women should be taught that many elements ought to be considered in choosing a mate. There are mutual likes and dislikes, effects of likes and dislikes, etc.

e. Role of personality. By only two persons were questions asked relative to personality (called temperament by the students) and these two were women.

FRESHMAN
Is it possible for two people of opposite temperaments to be happy together?

SENIOR
Should man and woman of entirely different temperaments and tastes be married if they love each other?

ALUMNI
No comment.

f. Role of religion, race, and nationality. The factors of religious, racial, and national differences appealed to many freshmen and seniors as very real barriers to marital happiness.

FRESHMEN
Is it wise to marry a girl of different nationality or religion?

How can religious differences be overcome?

Respect for religion if they happen to differ; or, whether or not they should have the same religion.

Are religious differences sufficient reason to refuse to marry? What are the proportions in which such marriages succeed?

SENIORS
Intermarriage of races, religions.

To what extent should religious differences be considered? Should this consideration be made before or after marriage?

How to arrange a satisfactory marriage between people of opposite religion?

What chances has a mixed marriage of succeeding, that is, two persons who are of different religions? In what religion should the children be brought up?

ALUMNI
No comment.

g. Role of age differential. The role of age differential evoked comment from undergraduate and alumni groups. Freshmen and alumni showed concern over the age problem when men marry women older than themselves. Seniors failed to make specific comment in this connection.

FRESHMEN

Should a man marry an older woman?

The ages of man and wife. How much difference should there be for a happy marriage?

How great a difference in ages should there be at the time of marriage?

SENIORS

The question of disparity of age and its effects on married life.

Should the boy's age be within three years of the girl's to make a happier and more successful marriage?

ALUMNUS

The bugaboo of differences in ages, wife several years older than husband.

h. Role of love. The importance of love as a guiding force in choosing a mate received comment from all groups. Most persons placed their comments in the form of questions. The statements of two are quoted to show how some expressed with certainty opposing convictions on the role of love. One freshman went on record as saying, "The most important thing, of course, is whether the two involved love each other," while an alumnus vigorously demanded that ". . . colleges ought to smash the myth that marriage is justified only if the two 'love each other.'"

FRESHMEN

Is love by both individuals necessary for a successful marriage?

Should couples marry if they do not experience a true love, only a need for companionship.

The most important thing, of course, is whether the two involved love each other. No marriage is secure without this.

SENIORS

The relative importance of romance in choosing a mate—how much love? How much cold appraisal?

Is it possible to have standards to go by in picking a wife and not depend wholly on love? And can one direct his love towards the suitable type of woman?

How much should sentimental affection or "love" influence the choosing of a life partner? Should it be all that? or should it be a choice purely of comparison of interest, companionship, like social status, financial, etc.?

ALUMNI

Is love necessary to marriage happiness?

I think the question of how to select a wife or husband is not a ridiculous one. I think that colleges ought to smash the myth that marriage is justified only if the two "love" each other regardless of other consideration. We should be taught to look in a mate for good health, good habits, fundamental soundness of character, well-balanced emotions and mentality as well as that thing called "love."

i. Role of infatuation. All groups showed an interest in finding means of differentiating between temporary infatuation and enduring love.

FRESHMEN

How can one differentiate between infatuation and love before it is too late?

How can you tell whether you're really in love enough so that your marriage will be successful?

How can you tell whether your love for a person is not just passion? Even if you stay in love for two or three years before marrying, it can die quickly after marriage. Why is that? How can it be determined before marriage whether your partner is the right one?

SENIORS

How can one tell whether he loves a member of the opposite sex or is it merely attraction which may be just temporary?

How can one differentiate between the physical attraction (infatuation) and the spiritual (love)?

ALUMNI

It should be pointed out that it is important before considering marriage to consider general compatibility other than the bliss of new romance.

Discussion of qualities to be desired in a wife or husband, keeping in mind the fleeting importance of an infatuation.

j. How to know if choice is the right one. The younger people participating in the study frequently asked questions dealing with the wise choice of a mate.

FRESHMAN

How to be sure you are choosing the right mate for a life of marriage?

SENIOR

The very first question I'd like to have answered is how does one know when he has chosen the right mate? To me this is a very important problem to be settled before the marriage ceremony takes place.

ALUMNI
No comment.

B. *When to Marry*

When to marry was a vital issue open to much debate. Undergraduate students and alumni asked: "Which is of greater importance to successful marriage, biological readiness or economic security?" It was evident that the college boy or girl wanted marriage but had no assurance of economic independence; the alumni wanted marriage but were not sufficiently established professionally; and many faced the choice between individual right to happiness and duty to family. The difficulties and conflicts of delayed marriage were focal points of concern.

Questions and comments dealing with the topic of when to marry fell into four sub-groups: (1) desirable age for marriage, (2) marriage before or after graduation, (3) time span between engagement and marriage, and (4) establishment in vocation before marriage. Eighty-one freshmen, 25 seniors, and four alumni gave suggestions in this general area.

1. *Desirable age for marriage*

Many more freshmen than seniors or alumni asked questions concerning desirable age for marriage. It is interesting that the nearer a subject approaches the socially accepted age for marriage, the less concerned he appears to be, unless his problem is complicated by pressures leading to delayed marriage.

FRESHMEN
I want a good answer to the question how old I should be to marry.

What is the best age for marriage from the viewpoint of both physical and mental maturity?

It seems that those who want to enter into matrimony have to wait so long because of economic conditions that much happiness is kept from them too long or lost altogether. What chances are there for happiness if a couple marries when young but doesn't enter into housekeeping until financially able?

SENIOR
What age, do statistics reveal, is the most ideal for marriage?

ALUMNUS
Should a man or woman get married before he or she reaches the age of thirty regardless of whether he or she has steady work?

2. *Marriage before or after graduation*

This is obviously a problem of undergraduate concern.

FRESHMAN
Another question on my mind—Should students marry? What advantages are there, if any, and what are the disadvantages?

SENIOR
Do college people settle down and get more out of college if they are married?

ALUMNI
No comment.

3. *Time span between engagement and marriage*

The technicalities of courtship do not appear to worry alumni. Freshmen appear to be interested in observing formalities. They are looking ahead, however, to at least three more years of college work, a real barrier to marriage which many desire but cannot achieve while still undergraduates.

FRESHMEN
How long should a courtship ending in marriage last?

How long should persons be engaged and what does this engagement mean?

SENIOR
Short vs. long engagements as contributing to successful marriage.

ALUMNI
No comment.

4. *Establishment in vocation before marriage*

In so far as the time for marriage depends upon the success of one's vocational career, it becomes a major and immediate concern of alumni. The problem is whether the college graduate dare marry as soon as he has finished school, when he knows nothing of his professional future, or whether he should wait until he is definitely established professionally.

FRESHMAN
Should college graduates marry as soon as they graduate, depending upon their education to secure them a job, or wait until they are settled and are earning enough to support a partner in marriage?

SENIOR
If I engage in professional study and am not self-sustaining would it affect my chances for success if I married?

ALUMNI
Should one marry as soon as he has fallen in love or should he wait until he has established himself in an adequate vocation?

Another question to think about is "When should a person marry?" Should he be definitely started on a career or can marriages be successful which are made in the floundering years right after graduation when, in these times of economic turmoil, even a college graduate has difficulty sometimes in starting on the work for which he has prepared himself?

C. Courtship Adjustments

Suggestions dealing with courtship adjustments were classified under the sub-groups: (1) questions to be discussed before marriage, (2) physical examination before marriage, (3) how to prepare for marriage, and (4) desirable relationships during courtship. On these subjects 42 freshmen, 26 seniors, and seven alumni gave comments or questions.

1. Questions to be discussed before marriage

In this sub-group few specific items were suggested. Both undergraduate students and alumni seemed to feel premarriage frankness was valuable; yet aside from deciding upon the number of children, few suggestions were offered. Freshmen, particularly, stressed the idea of decision as to number of children during the courtship period.

FRESHMAN
How should young couples intending to get married get to the point and discuss children, beliefs, etc.?

SENIOR
Advisability of complete premarriage frankness between husband and wife.

ALUMNUS
Such important questions as to the number of children should be solved before entering marriage. It seems to me that a planned family life would certainly be a more happy one than one which was not planned.

2. *Physical examination before marriage*

General interest was apparent in questions dealing with premarital physical examinations.

FRESHMAN

A medical examination should be included in the requirements to obtain a marriage license. This would aid both the individual and society.

SENIOR

Should both parties in a proposed marriage subject themselves to a rigid physical examination?

ALUMNUS

Whether or not it is a good idea for young couples to have medical examinations before marriage.

3. *How to prepare for marriage*

There seemed to be a desire for proper preparation for marriage. Seniors stressed the point more than freshmen and alumni. Seniors particularly were interested in forcing the partners in marriage to recognize the realities of life.

FRESHMAN

One of the most important things that both parties involved should know is the true meaning of this common bondage, marriage. They should know what the other wishes to get out of married life.

SENIOR

The necessity for debunking so many of our romantic illusions, and replacing them with the realities of work, mutual respect, readjustment, etc.

ALUMNUS

Teaching and explaining the rising problems of young folks when financial or in-law problems are involved in forthcoming marriage plans.

4. *Desirable relationship during courtship*

All groups seemed to want to know the procedures for wisely conducted courtship.

FRESHMAN

What are the proper relationships during the period of courtship?

SENIOR

What should two parties learn about each other during engagement?

ALUMNUS

Preparation for marriage, what courtship period and engagement should mean?

D. *Youth Relationships*

Suggestions dealing with youth relations were classified under the sub-groups: (1) how to attract and win regard of other sex, (2) getting along with other young people, and (3) social life—amount, kind, standards of behavior. On these subjects 25 freshmen, 16 seniors, and five alumni gave suggestions.

In the area of relationships between young people of opposite sexes the interests of freshmen and seniors appeared to parallel one another. In both instances personal emotional doubts and agitations seemed to evoke the questioning. On the other hand, alumni tended to see youth relationships more or less as an undergraduate problem of general adjustment, e.g., "College men and women should be taught how to overcome social maladjustments, ways of preventing social unstability."

1. How to attract and win regard of other sex

There seemed to be little difference in the interests of freshmen and seniors on this point. Alumni failed to comment.

FRESHMEN

Does a girl have to neck to be popular in college?

How can you win the love of the certain person whose love you desire?

SENIORS

How to make yourself more attractive to the opposite sex.

How can a man keep a girl interested in him? Should a technique of courtship and lovemaking be developed, or is sincerity sufficient?

ALUMNI

No comment.

2. Getting along with other young people

Alumni stressed the importance of getting along with other people more than did undergraduates. Freshmen failed to comment.

FRESHMEN

No comment.

SENIOR

Instruction in how to "get along" with other people should also be included.

ALUMNI

Perhaps one of the most important matters to be considered in such a course is the art of getting along with other people. It seems to me that the individual who gets along well with his roommate in college, his classmates, his brothers and sisters, must have qualities which will make him live harmoniously with a husband or wife and with his children.

College men and women ought to be able to understand the feelings and emotions of their associates. They should learn to respect the ideals of others and try to sort out the better from the good ones.

3. Social life—amount, kind, standards of behavior

To some students the regulation of one's social life appears to be a definite problem—particularly to those with limited financial backing.

FRESHMEN

How much of the student's time should be occupied with social and recreational activities as compared with study?

Can a boy or girl work his way through college and still get the most out of it?

Should you run around with sons of rich families while you yourself would like to but your father says he can't afford it. How to refuse their invitations politely.

SENIORS

Do you really believe a student should try to work his way through college without entering into any social activities such as dances, plays, and so forth?

Is it advisable to go "steady" with just one girl or go with every girl you can date?

Money questions between sweethearts. Many times the boy is poor and cannot afford the good times that other fellows can offer the girl; what arrangements can be made here?

ALUMNUS

Friends: best type and how to meet.

IV. SEX

Questions dealing with sex were suggested by 298 freshmen, 229 seniors, and 138 alumni. What challenged one class, challenged all. Certain marked lines of thinking and similarity of problems could be followed throughout comments and questions of all groups. Suggestions in this category were classified under the headings: (A) General

Sex Education, (B) Sex Education of Children, (C) Venereal Disease, (D) Psychology of Sex, (E) Premarital Sex Adjustments, (F) Marital Adjustments, (G) Prevention of Conception, and (H) Prostitution, Trial and Companionate Marriage.

A. General Sex Education

Under general sex education were classified items that fell into two sub-groups: (1) amount and kind, and (2) reproduction, anatomy, physiology. On this subject 67 freshmen, 59 seniors, and 61 alumni commented. It may be recalled that 51 per cent of the entire group of participants were freshmen.

1. Amount and kind of sex education

There was a heavy demand from freshmen, seniors, and alumni for specific information pertaining to sex. The insistence seemed as determined in one group as another.

FRESHMEN
Might more adequate sex education be effective in improving family relations as well as other relations?

Thorough instruction about the sexual functionings of our bodies.

Give some information regarding the problem of thoroughly understanding the underlying and fundamental motives of sex.

SENIORS
I believe a course in marital hygiene and physiology would be of great value. It would clear up the many questions the average young person has regarding marriage.

More unabridged, unveiled sex education.

Provide some practical sex education, not the stories about the bees and the flowers that Christian Associations give us.

ALUMNI
Physiology and anatomy to familiarize students with the human body so as to further sympathy and understanding between man and woman.

Because of the temper of the college group, it seems to me that problems involving sexual adjustment—whatever we may think of their intrinsic significance—are of first importance. A free and candid discussion, with someone who knows, is what most students need.

A sturdy, clean course in shall we say sex technique without the good Doctor's horror stories and pictures, without clothing the whole in such a manner as to make the whole matter devolve upon some poor little spirochaetes and diplococci. Teach them the normality of sex and its various manifestations. Teach the proper techniques in both courtship and marriage. Teach them cleanliness—not smut. And, perhaps, a little side excursion into a few abnormalities—to round off the picture.

2. *Reproduction, anatomy, physiology*

Under the heading reproduction, anatomy, physiology, the quality of question asked and the type of information demanded were very much alike for all groups.

FRESHMAN
More instruction on the biological functions especially those pertaining to the physical relationship.

SENIOR
There should be more time spent on the functions and the purposes of the sex organs.

ALUMNUS
Young individuals should be taught the anatomy and physiology of the sex organs.

B. *Sex Education of Children*

On the subject of sex education for children, 15 freshmen, eight seniors, and two alumni gave questions or comments.

FRESHMEN
How can parents inform their children on sex and its problems efficiently, sensibly, and so they can understand?

Sex instruction for children, what age to start, how much to tell them, and what particular aspects to tell them.

SENIORS
An intimate and intelligent way to educate one's children in sexual knowledge.

When should specific sex instruction be given to the child? Should it be given by father to son and mother to daughter? or should there be no differentiation?

ALUMNI
Questions should be answered (by parents) by virtue of the very fact that they have been asked, and not put off with, "You are too young" or "You should not ask such questions of your parents."

To get at the root of this whole business of sex education the future parents (i.e., the college students of today) should be taught the importance of beginning sex education in their children as soon as they can talk well enough to ask questions—not as formal instruction but as freely answered questions. After all, abnormal eroticism and suppression are practically synonymous.

C. Venereal Disease

Some interest was expressed in the subject of venereal disease. The type of question asked was more or less uniform throughout all groups. Twenty-one freshmen, 16 seniors, and nine alumni asked questions or gave suggestions in this area.

FRESHMAN
Venereal diseases, treatment and prevention.

SENIOR
I think youth should be informed about transmittable disorders which would affect offspring.

ALUMNUS
They should be taught the dangers of venereal diseases and how to avoid them.

D. Psychology of Sex

Items dealing with the psychology of sex were classified in two sub-groups, (1) understanding other sex, and (2) psychology of sex life. On this subject 10 freshmen, eight seniors, and eight alumni commented.

1. Understanding other sex

There appears to be a mutuality of desire on the part of all groups for an understanding of the differences between ways of thinking and feeling of men and women.

FRESHMAN
I feel also that basic courses in the psychology of marriage should be offered. Men and women are essentially different in most of their attitudes toward life, and some ways should be accounted for which would make these attitudes harmonize more nearly. I believe a great many marriages have failed because men do not understand women as personalities and vice versa.

SENIOR
Consideration of differences between male and female psychology.

ALUMNUS

A new course (co-ed) dealing with the idiosyncracies of man's and woman's mind. This might fall under a psychology heading, but I'd be inclined to believe that a professor would like to make it too technical. What the aim should be is to put this in commonplace language so you don't have to be a student of the subject before you can get anything out of the course.

2. Psychology of sex life

The same unanimity of desire for information appears among the comments on the psychology of sex as has been seen in other topics related to sex.

FRESHMAN

What is the psychology of a suitable sex life after marriage and how should it be treated?

SENIOR

There should be much psychology in the course. We would like to study the effects which men and women have upon each other in the marital relationship so we would know better what to avoid.

ALUMNUS

I believe that the greatest step that colleges can be making during the students' four years toward the preparation of young men and women to solve their family and personal problems is the free and frank education in matters of sex—the philosophy and psychology of the significance of the human sexual nature.

E. Premarital Sex Adjustments

Suggestions dealing with premarital sex adjustments were classified under the headings: (1) desirable boy-girl sex relationships, and (2) control of sex impulse of the unmarried. On these subjects 53 freshmen, 38 seniors, and 10 alumni gave comments or questions.

1. Desirable boy-girl sex relationships

The alumnus quoted below seems to have put his finger upon the reason for the uncertainty of values which ran through the comments of undergraduates.

FRESHMAN

What to do (or not) in courtship for best results and happiness in marriage later on.

SENIOR

Instruction in courtship should enumerate good and bad types of practices: what is proper and what is not.

ALUMNUS

Chastity before marriage. The problem has been much discussed of late, an article appearing in the recent Readers Digest. While in college the problem did not present itself because I was too busy with other things, and because at that time it was a settled question in my mind. Lately, however, when so many young people are overstepping the bounds of chastity and the moral stigma of unchastity is falling away, it presents a problem which I have had to think over and solve anew.

2. Control of sex impulse of unmarried

The comments submitted by freshmen, seniors, and alumni suggest that control of the sex impulse of the unmarried and questions of premarital chastity are two aspects of one problem. There appeared definite emotional conflict among undergraduates where sex life must be thwarted because of factors for which the persons involved were not responsible. The alumni approach was somewhat less colored by emotion.

FRESHMEN

How can two average young people who are in love and cannot be married for a few years keep from, or at least control, satisfaction of sexual impulses?

If marriage is not financially possible, what is the substitute, if any?

A frank treatment of sexual desires and emotions; also ways of satisfying them would be welcomed.

SENIORS

The question of what young people should do before marriage in the case where prolonged acquaintance with members of the opposite sex makes sexual abstinence impossible.

Recognition and group discussion of problems of unmarried.

To my mind the problem of premarital satisfaction of the sexual impulse is all-important.

ALUMNI

They should be taught how to convert sexual energy into suitable channels.

I believe every young man and woman should learn, even at adolescence, about sex and the sex urge. They should be taught that it is a natural thing and when controlled will help make living a more pleasant business.

Sex life before marriage; sex life of single.

F. Marital Adjustments

Suggestions dealing with marital adjustments were classified under the headings: (1) sex adjustments in marriage, (2) childbirth, (3) extra-marital relations, and (4) importance of sex in marriage. Questions and comments were received from 79 freshmen, 46 seniors, and 24 alumni.

1. Sex adjustments in marriage

The prevailing feeling among all groups seemed to be that happy marriage depends greatly upon sexual adjustment between man and woman and that any maladjustments which occur might have been avoided had the persons involved received before marriage full information relative to the nature of sex relationships between husband and wife.

FRESHMEN

The question dealing with sexual congeniality in married life should be dealt with more extensively and with less restraint.

How can sexual intercourse be indulged in so as to give maximum satisfaction, benefit, and enjoyment?

SENIORS

It seems to me that colleges attempting to sponsor worthwhile courses on marital life should include questions dealing with the physical or sexual relationships of an adjusted happy marriage. If the hygienic slant were sensibly given to all college students, there would be fewer sexual irregularities in the college generation and more whole marriages.

How to get the most enjoyment, sexual and spiritual, out of marriage.

ALUMNI

This course should include a frank discussion of the problems likely to confront a married couple in relation to the adjustment of their sex life, and an effort to impress on them the urgency of an immediate and satisfactory adjustment of such problems, and to point out to them the available sources of guidance on such problems.

College is definitely the place to learn that physical living together is an art just as social intercourse, and is based on the same principles of cooperation and understanding of the other person's nature and problems.

2. Childbirth

This subject brought forth only two comments, one from a freshman and one from an alumnus:

FRESHMAN
Facts concerning the birth of children.

ALUMNUS
While women have a matter-of-fact interest in the subject of childbirth experience, men have a tendency to have a sentimental dread of it.

3. Extra-marital relations

Only slight interest was revealed in the subject of extra-marital relations. Some comment, however, was forthcoming from all groups.

FRESHMAN
What will be the result of any intimate relations with men or women outside of marriage?

SENIOR
In case of illness or incompatibility of sex satisfaction of husband or wife, should one visit or associate with others to satisfy the sex desire?

ALUMNUS
Nature should not be suppressed but rather should it be intelligently guided. We can't make all marriages successful but we can attempt to lessen the number of failures and of sexual maladjustment and promiscuity.

4. Importance of sex in marriage

A proper evaluation of the importance of sex as a factor in successful marriage was demanded by freshmen, seniors, and alumni.

FRESHMAN
Is the much heralded sex as much a factor in a successful marriage as it is said to be?

SENIOR
How important is sex in the successful marriage?

ALUMNUS
The sex factor in marriage. Its real meaning and possibilities.

G. Prevention of Conception

Suggestions dealing with prevention of conception were classified in the sub-groups: (1) techniques of contraception, (2) ethics of contraception, (3) spacing and number of children. On these subjects 46 freshmen, 50 seniors, and 21 alumni expressed themselves.

1. Techniques of contraception

Many freshmen, seniors and alumni appeared to believe that information relative to contraceptive methods would not only be valuable but necessary.

FRESHMAN
What are the best methods of contraception and what are the virtues?

SENIOR
The use of contraceptive methods. The values of the various types and the evils, if any.

ALUMNUS
A thorough knowledge of contraceptives, their relative merits and ways of obtaining them would be of great help to young brides with no sounder judgment to consult than "the girl down the hall."

2. Ethics of contraception

Many freshmen and seniors seemed uncertain about the ethics of contraception. Some of these uncertainties were traceable to the teachings of the Church; others were based upon moral factors. Ethical considerations did not seem to trouble many alumni.

FRESHMAN
I am a Roman Catholic, and I find it hard to reconcile the view of the Church on sex, birth control, etc., with the prevalent worldly and seemingly logical views of today. Therefore, I'd like a little clear-headed thinking done for me on this problem. Naturally a wife and a husband would have to hold the same views on this problem, and I'm wondering how we'd straighten it out if I, with the worldly masculine viewpoint on sexual relations, should marry a girl who had been reared a strict Catholic and held exactly opposite views to mine. I don't agree with my Church and yet its arguments still hold some weight with me and prevent me from agreeing with the strictly modern thinkers.

SENIOR
Changing moral conceptions of the birth control question.

ALUMNUS
I also am firmly convinced that the question of birth control is another important issue and is becoming more so daily. This important problem should be given a foremost position in the movement relating to personal problems and family relationships.

3. Spacing and number of children

While the subject of the spacing and number of children drew forth a limited number of responses, there were representatives from freshman, senior, and alumni groups who asked for information.

FRESHMEN
Is it possible to plan when to have children so that neither career nor finances will be in the way?

Is it possible to limit the number of children? How?

SENIORS
Education in the spacing of children?

Should young couples have large families in times of economic insecurity? If not, why not extend birth control clinics for both physical and educational aid? Are not abortions wise in many cases?

ALUMNI
Birth control, when and if possible, with the accepted figures on relation of children to income, spacing age of children.

In my own experience and in that of others, there ought to be more education in colleges on the size of a family and how to regulate it. In my opinion, not much can be done until both husband and wife have had the advantage of education. Just the education brings tolerance.

H. Prostitution, Trial and Companionate Marriage

The response to the subjects prostitution and trial and companionate marriage was slight. Only seven freshmen, four seniors, and three alumni commented in this area. However, suggestions were forthcoming from all groups.

1. Prostitution

There were only occasional questions which dealt with the problem of prostitution.

FRESHMAN
Are occasional visits to disorderly homes really as detrimental as is said?

SENIOR
Should prostitution and sterilization be legal?

ALUMNUS
The why's and wherefore's of prostitution and casual sex relations should be studied and thus discouraged.

2. Trial and companionate marriage

Suggestions and questions concerning trial and companionate marriage were infrequent.

FRESHMAN
Isn't companionate marriage a wise thing? that is to live with a man for a certain length of time to make sure you are willing to live with him the rest of your life?

SENIOR
What about trial or companionate marriage?

ALUMNUS
Free love; companionate marriage.

V. ACCORD IN FAMILY ADJUSTMENT (EXCLUDING SEX)

The questions dealing with the non-sexual adjustments of family life seemed to fall into two groups—accord and discord, positive and negative aspects of the dynamics of adjustment. Whether approached positively or negatively the issue was the same, namely, how to sustain satisfying adjustments in marriage. "How to have perfect happiness with your wife or husband" and "Are divorces the only answer to family trouble?" are merely two different approaches to the same goal of harmonious family living. This section deals with the questions on accord and Section VI with questions on discord.

Suggestions dealing with accord in family adjustment were classified under the headings: (A) Personal Husband-Wife Relations, (B) Leisure and Outside Interests, (C) Psychology of Adjustment, (D) General Family Relationships, (E) Domination and Control, and (F) Member Role. On these topics 131 freshmen, 131 seniors, and 124 alumni asked questions or gave suggestions.

A. Personal Husband-Wife Relations

Suggestions in this area were classified in four sub-groups: (1) early marriage, (2) growth of mutual understanding, (3) confidences, privacy, and (4) permanence of marriage. On this subject 53 freshmen, 44 seniors, and 15 alumni commented.

1. Early marriage

Freshmen, seniors, and alumni all seemed aware that the cross-currents of early marriage call for adjustments and sacrifices by both partners in the new relationship.

FRESHMAN
When a man and woman get married, there are many changes they must make in their lives. They could be taught how to accustom themselves to married life.

SENIOR
Anything that would tend to ease those first few years of marriage—to tide over those periods of stress and storm until love and understanding can permanently bridge the gap.

ALUMNUS
Probably the first big problem in married life is to learn to adjust one's self to husband or wife.

2. *Growth of mutual understanding*

There seemed to be among freshmen, seniors, and alumni alike a fairly realistic attitude toward potential dangers in early marriage but a genuine desire on the part of all for help in fostering the development of mutual understanding.

FRESHMEN
What can we do to make ourselves sufficiently interesting so that we may be able to keep the interest of our mate, husband or wife?

How can love grow deeper through the years? Methods of keeping each other's love.

SENIORS
Suggestions and aids for improvement of later marital life after the "romance" has died and the prosaic duties of everyday life begin to weigh on one.

What must be done by one to retain the love and admiration of the other? How can two people best grow together after marriage?

ALUMNI
The ability to distinguish a problem of adjustment from a definite break in relationships.

On the whole college men and women are ultimately planning on marriage. Practically a universal question they are asking is, "How can we stay happily married?"

In connection with marital relationships it might be possible in formal courses to stress the need for sympathetic understanding of and tolerance for the shortcomings of one's chosen partner and the recognition of one's own shortcomings.

3. *Confidences and privacy*

The subject of confidences and privacy was a matter of concern only to freshmen and seniors. However, from an alumnus there was a demand for the observance of etiquette between husband and wife relative to their individual rights.

FRESHMEN

Is frankness and truth always to be desired in marriage?

Should there be secrets between husband and wife?

SENIORS

Should a wife or a husband still keep a certain amount of privacy physically, mentally. That is, how much as a rule does marriage influence attitudes and relations? Why?

Should one always tell the truth to one's mate? or is it better to keep things hidden because at the moment they may cause an argument?

ALUMNUS

Etiquette (rights of each, privileges, single and double standards after as well as before marriage).

4. Permanence of marriage

The desire for lasting happiness from one's marriage is a constant factor in all groups.

FRESHMAN

Does love exist for years after a couple is married and how can it be retained and treasured?

SENIOR

The necessity for companionship in a real marriage and for close and intimate relationships aside from the physical one should be stressed.

ALUMNUS

They should discuss and think through the problem of how to develop a spiritual, lasting relationship between husband and wife. Somehow it would help if they could learn to avoid the little angles, little misunderstandings.

B. Leisure and Outside Interests

Comments and questions concerning leisure and outside interests fell into three sub-groups: (1) shared interests, (2) outside contacts of individual family members, and (3) family community contacts. On this subject 11 freshmen, 23 seniors, and 22 alumni commented.

1. Shared interests

Freshmen suggestions in this area seemed limited in scope and focused on the pleasure to be had for the family. Seniors and alumni more often regarded shared interests as a means to family solidarity.

FRESHMEN
What form of recreation can the family as a whole participate in?

In order to have a satisfying family and successful marriage, people should be taught to live together and appreciate one another. The reason for a great many unsuccessful marriages is that either one of the persons—or probably both—are too interested in worldly activities. If this is the case, there will be little or no family life. This could be eliminated if the husband and wife would share their social responsibilities with those of their family.

SENIORS
Finding and emphasizing common mental interests and objectives: also common recreational interests so as to grow closer socially and mentally.

After a couple have been married and find out that their interests are vastly different, are there any ways by which they can make an adjustment so that they can be more happy and enjoy things together?

ALUMNI
Stepping to a more objective plan, I should like to counsel education in the use of leisure time, for the sake both of father and mother in their declining years, and of son and daughter in their formative ones. Nothing can cement a family, separated by disparate ages and interests as can common hobbies and leisure activities beyond a mere jaunt to a movie or a seat beside the radio.

To be able to find relaxation and enjoyment in each other's company is the most important thing to me—and the biggest contributing factor to this is a sense of humor. It's a lot of fun to laugh and play together and it establishes a mutual sympathetic understanding that even surpasses that accomplished through the sexual union.

2. *Outside contacts of individual family members*

Few questions were asked relative to the outside contacts of individual family members, yet all groups were represented by suggestions.

FRESHMAN
Is it right for a wife to expect her husband to give up recreations such as fishing or hunting because she wants him to? Shouldn't she try to learn them instead?

SENIOR
Do you think that short vacations in which the husband and wife go separate ways will relieve the monotony of married life and cause fewer divorces?

ALUMNUS
Specifically, how much freedom of movement and association shall I encourage in my wife? If wives are intelligent, they will want some part in the great social drama of today. How can this be achieved with a minimum of danger to the home I hope to have?

3. Family community contacts

On this subject freshmen made no comment. While seniors recognized to a certain extent the responsibility of the family to the community, their vision seemed less broad than that of alumni.

FRESHMEN
No comment.

SENIORS
Relation of your family to the family next door—your part and theirs.
To what extent should neighborhood or community social life distract from home life? a. Before children. b. After children.

ALUMNI
The home and community life.
I think also that an attempt should be made to impress each individual with the duty of the family to participate in the life of the community. In every phase of community life, social, political, religious and educational, the family by assuming its share of responsibility can exercise its influence for bettering the life of the nation. This can only be achieved by the action of each individual as a member of the family.

C. Psychology of Adjustment

Items suggested on topics in the area of the psychology of family adjustment fell into three sub-groups: (1) personal and family psychology, (2) mental hygiene, and (3) personality and character development. On this subject 13 freshmen, 16 seniors, and 29 alumni commented. It is interesting to observe the relatively large response in this area and in general family relationships from alumni who represented only 23 per cent of the total group.

1. Personal and family psychology

On this subject one finds generalizations from freshmen, seniors, and alumni.

FRESHMEN
Helpful instruction on the psychological side of marriage.
Review of marriage psychology, e.g., trust in each other, consideration for each other, "team" attitude and ambitions.

SENIORS
Psychology and its application in promoting better mutual understanding and consideration in marriage.

An attempt to analyze a little more accurately, if possible, the phenomenon of genuine adult love in order to prevent costly marital mistakes—a psychological investigation.

ALUMNUS
Courses in psychology (or sociology) not from the academic standpoint of "defining a reflex arc" or knowing what a threshold stimulus is, but as a tool to be used. Teach the matter so that it is vital, not distressingly physiological or beautifully didactic. Show them the whys and wherefores of simpler behavior patterns, teach them to analyze motives, acts, adjustments in marriage from the practical side.

2. Mental hygiene

Freshmen, seniors, and alumni all felt a need for instruction in mental hygiene as a means of preserving stability.

FRESHMAN
Some elemental mental hygiene.

SENIOR
A detailed study of ways and means to preserve one's mental health throughout the whole of one's married life.

ALUMNUS
We need security and maturity. Any way we can learn to understand our motivations will help us decide with reason and to adjust ourselves to the situation we are in. No course in college is going to make secure and well-integrated individuals out of the hodge-podge of emotions of those who will sign up for it, but if we could intellectually see the danger points we might have strength enough to combat the emotions.

3. Personality and character development

Only a slight interest was shown in this subject. Each group was represented by very few questions.

FRESHMAN
What are the probable effects of married life on character?

SENIOR
How does married life affect one's personality and in what way may these changes be modified to cope with the social order in which one is living?

ALUMNUS
Make them understand their own personalities. Ask them what they want from life . . . and then try (I said try) to show them some of the hurdles they will have to meet.

D. General Family Relationships

Suggestions emphasizing general family relationships fell into four sub-groups: (1) family relations, general, (2) role of tolerance, con-

sideration of others, understanding, (3) duties and responsibilities of
family members, and (4) developing harmony, success, stability. On
this subject 29 freshmen, 33 seniors, and 49 alumni commented.

1. Family relations—general

The greater number of questions on the subject of general family
relations came from the older groups, seniors and alumni, rather than
from freshmen. The statements tended to be quite general and philosophical in emphasis.

FRESHMAN
Give students an idea what life is about, what constitutes happiness, what
to strive for, and what not to strive for. What are the important things in
the end.

SENIOR
I believe that we should try to reach some conclusion for the furtherance of
a more stable family life. Why do people marry, and, after marriage, what
happens to the unity, happiness and harmony that the couple promise to
uphold? I believe this move is a wonderful one. It is necessary if we wish
to maintain the primary group of our society.

ALUMNUS
The purposes and functions of personal discipline in our relations to family
and from that to our community and state, should find some place in every
person's life.

2. Role of tolerance, consideration of others, understanding

The one freshman comment in this area is rather wordy, but the
underlying thought appears to correspond with that of seniors and
alumni on the same subject.

FRESHMAN
In my opinion one of the primary difficulties of early marital life is the lack
of consideration which college graduates show for their partners and, primarily, marriage is a partnership. College graduates are usually self-
centered individuals whose foremost considerations are for the ego. This
inflated ego often leads to the destruction of an otherwise successful marriage. The refusal to consider your partner's viewpoint does, I believe, lead
to difficulties which become more and more serious and lead to disastrous
results.

SENIOR
Instruction in how to be cooperative and unselfish in the home.

ALUMNUS
Social virtues such as consideration, sympathy, willingness to help, and self-
restraint must be emphasized and cultivated in any system of premarital
guidance.

3. Duties and responsibilities of family members

Some concern was expressed by members of all groups for responsibility to other members of the family.

FRESHMAN
How can I live my life to the fullest that not only I but also my family may benefit from the results of my living?

SENIOR
Next I think we could stand some training in meeting situations which come up in marriage. What the duties of the husband and wife are to each other and to themselves.

ALUMNUS
One of the most important things that should be taught in the class suggested is that true affection or love of any sort should be based upon mutual respect and that parents must earn such respect from their children and give it in return.

4. Developing harmony, success, and stability

The small number of freshmen, seniors, and alumni who suggested items in this area seemed to realize that for the family to have harmony, success, and stability each individual must make his contribution.

FRESHMAN
How to learn to analyze a person's mind in order to be able to get along with that certain person.

SENIOR
An emphasis on Burgess' definition of the family—"A group of interacting personalities"—so there will be some measure of understanding about the reactions of two people who must work and play together harmoniously.

ALUMNUS
Concluding thought—the family unit is seldom perfect. There is a definite amount of give-and-take. The college trained must in many cases elevate the family plane or in turn, failing, lose his own personality.

E. Domination and Control

The subject of domination and control was divided into two subgroups representing different approaches to the same problem: (1) authoritarianism, and (2) democratic adjustments. Seventeen freshmen, 12 seniors, and seven alumni gave suggestions that dealt with these topics.

1. *Authoritarianism*

It was the freshmen who more often felt the need for a well-defined understanding of who should control the family.

FRESHMEN

Is it essential that either husband or wife predominate in household affairs?

How should the institution of marriage be managed? Should it be a 50–50 proposition or should there be one boss of the family?

How much "say" should each (husband and wife) have over the other?

SENIORS

Should there be any question of dominance in the family or should there be practical equalization?

Should there be a dominant and recessive relationship between husband and wife?

ALUMNI

College women feel they have a productive value and to be treated as a housekeeper is too much to swallow. Can you teach prospective mothers and fathers that both have invested equally in the marriage business? Both to reap, not just the male. Above all, let this course be coeducational. It *was* a man's world. Women's intrusion has built up a competitive angle that can't be ignored. It is my belief that harmony must be established if we are to be a great nation. The foundation lies in the home.

Females should be taught to share responsibilities and not hide behind the skirts of their sex.

2. *Democratic adjustments*

Interest in democratic adjustments within the family were expressed by members of each group.

FRESHMAN

In a successful marriage should not the husband and wife have everything 50–50, each admit the other's equal intelligence and each have a share in the finances, etc.?

SENIOR

Are equalitarian marriages desirable? If so, what are some advantages? If not, what are some disadvantages?

ALUMNI

Finally it should be emphasized somewhere that marriage and home life is a proposition which requires, as someone told me, that both the man and woman go 75 per cent of the way. They should realize that patience and tolerance are required if little misunderstandings are not to wreck marital happiness.

They must be instructed in the necessity of mutual sharing of all the good and bad things of life. They must be taught that marriage is a partnership in which each has equal rights and equal responsibilities.

F. Member Role

The most pertinent comments under "member role" centered around the baby in the family: How are the adult members affected by its arrival? On this subject eight freshmen, three seniors, and two alumni commented.

FRESHMAN
What should be the attitude of a husband toward the arrival of a child? Should he be pushed into the background or are there things which he might do?

SENIOR
How is one to prevent one's husband from feeling he is "second fiddle" after a baby has arrived?

ALUMNUS
Sincerely believe that most fathers do not think of their place in the home (or the child's life) until a child arrives. Seems to me that a directed study of this question—in college—would have positive results.

VI. DISCORD (EXCLUDING SEX)

Suggestions dealing with the topic of discord were classified under the headings: (A) Divorce and Separation, (B) Factors Contributing to Discord, and (C) Resolving Conflict. On these subjects 48 freshmen, 45 seniors, and 12 alumni commented. When considering the problem of family adjustment, many more persons thought in terms of accord than of discord. This was particularly evident among alumni, the group in which the largest number were married.

A. Divorce and Separation

Questions on divorce and separation were classified in three subgroups: (1) divorce and separation—general, (2) causes, and (3) effects.

1. Divorce and separation—general

Under divorce and separation the questions covering general aspects of the subject outnumber those pertaining to the specific. Comment would indicate, in the main, acute awareness of the possibilities of divorce rather than close analysis of factors causing it.

FRESHMAN
What does all this incompatibility used so much in divorce cases include? How can divorces be given by this?

SENIOR
We must realize that the divorce trend in the United States has shown a definite and momentous increase. It is in my opinion important that the instruction include information and aid in this respect. . . . It is surprising to see and notice how many professional men and women are divorced.

ALUMNUS
I'm inclined to think that the American born man or woman looks to divorce as a safety factor. That is, they marry without looking ahead and depend on divorce to release them if they can not make a go of their united life.

2. *Causes*

Questions dealing with causes of discord were expressed in very general terms.

FRESHMAN
What is lacking in a family that breaks up in divorce courts?

SENIOR
Study of divorce in all aspects to determine what deficiencies in one or both members led to divorce.

ALUMNUS
A study of a series of case histories demonstrating the usual contributing factors to family discord and divorce would help. These are, of course, impossible to comprehend absolutely, but general classifications might be made.

3. *Effects*

Only freshmen commented on the general effects of divorce, and their concern seemed to be focused almost wholly upon the effect of divorce on the child of separated parents.

FRESHMEN
The divorce question: how to make your home life happy and successful when your parents are divorced and not have divorce spoil your conception of marriage.

Should families in which there are children consider divorce?

How is it possible for children to get along and lead a normal life when their parents are divorced?

SENIORS
No comment.

ALUMNI
No comment.

B. Factors Contributing to Discord

Factors contributing to discord fell into two groupings: (1) general causes of discord, and (2) role of specific factors. On this subject 11 freshmen, 17 seniors, and six alumni commented.

1. General causes of discord

Under this heading questions seemed to be directed at the home in process of disorganization rather than the home which had been broken by separation or divorce.

FRESHMAN
What are the common causes and probable cures for the breaking down of homes?

SENIOR
What are the pitfalls leading to unhappy marriages and divorce? How are they to be avoided?

ALUMNUS
The morals of marriage, treating such questions as validity of marriage vow, so-called freedom in marriage, drink, separation.

2. Role of specific factors

If a tabulation were made of the specific factors contributing to discord, which freshmen, seniors and alumni suggested, one would find in the list the most commonly recognized causes of discord. Only a few are mentioned in these illustrations.

FRESHMEN
Should financial matters rule family discord?

Is lack of control and selfish desire an important cause of unhappy marriage?

SENIORS
A course that will deal frankly with the problems that cause incompatibility in marriage, both physical and mental incompatibility, should be included.

Different religious and cultural viewpoints and possibilities therein for future disagreements leading to violent disturbances in the home.

ALUMNI

Some marriages are shipwrecked because of "little things." Perhaps a thorough course in wedded etiquette would smooth over rough places.

A thorough realization of the role of cause and effect in excesses, whether alcoholic, sexual or otherwise.

C. Resolving Conflict

This topic was divided into two sub-groups: (1) adjustment of conflict, and (2) sources of help in resolving discord. On this subject 13 freshmen, seven seniors, and one alumnus commented.

1. Adjustment of conflict

Adjustment of conflict within the family group was a matter of great concern to a small group of the participants.

FRESHMAN

How can family disagreements, if and when they arise, be corrected? Can family disagreements be avoided?

SENIOR

By what technique can the most unimportant quarrels be solved? (We should be able to generalize where small issues are concerned.)

ALUMNUS

Sometimes, through petty annoyances an emotional state arises which causes you to wonder why you ever got married in the first place and if a nice, painless divorce wouldn't be the wisest thing before there are any children to complicate the situation. But since you actually love the man, you know you are wrong.

2. Sources of help in resolving discord

Only seniors appeared interested in the use of outside agencies as a means of help in resolving family discord.

FRESHMEN

No comment

SENIORS

What sources are available to improve unsuccessful marriages, such as family courts and marriage clinics?

Analyses of phases of conflict and disorganization in the family, and possible ways to overcome or avoid them. Where get help?

ALUMNI

No comment.

VII. FAMILY ECONOMICS

Suggestions dealing with Family Economics were classified under the headings: (A) Budgeting, (B) Control, (C) Cost of Parenthood, (D) Savings, Insurance, Investment, (E) General Family Finance, (F) Wage-Earning Wife, and (G) Finances Necessary to Marry. On these topics 177 freshmen, 115 seniors, and 79 alumni expressed themselves.

A. Budgeting

Questions on budgeting fell into two sub-groups: (1) methods of budgeting, and (2) desirability of budgeting. On this subject 38 freshmen, 30 seniors, and 33 alumni commented. A heavy poll of questions was registered by all groups. Both men and women asked for instruction.

1. Methods of budgeting

Many of the young people expressed a keen desire to learn how to budget their incomes.

FRESHMEN
How does one go about making a complete budget of the family income?

Instruction on how to make and maintain an adequate budget.

How can the budget be well balanced?

SENIORS
How should a family starting out, budget a moderate income?

Questions on financial matters and how to keep them straight—making an efficient budget according to the income and keeping within it.

Should a young married couple buy all of their household furnishings at the start even though it means installment plans, or should they wait until they are situated better pecuniarily?

ALUMNI
A simple and flexible budget system.

A family budget—how to pare it to provide first for the necessary essentials and then take care of the luxuries.

Budgeting and sound economy in home management.

2. *Desirability of budgeting*

The conviction as to the value of a sound budget system was almost wholly positive. A comment suggesting a possible negative value was rare.

FRESHMAN
Is too careful budgeting detrimental to the family?

SENIORS
Veering off to another line, I also think that budgeting is essential. Men and women both must be taught the value of money and how to live within their means. Before marriage both have their own money to spend and cannot realize that now they have responsibilities.

ALUMNI
There are budget problems to be met. The capable management of a husband's salary results in smooth living. Restraint in spending and the careful allotment of funds is so necessary and so difficult to teach.

A definite help toward a more happy adult life might be gained through a study of how to live on a budget. In college few of us have to think of any sort of balance between income and expenditures which, of course, is an absolute essential in later life if one is to be happy and contented.

B. *Control*

Suggestions on control of family economics centered around two aspects of the same problem, the allocation of authority in family finance as contrasted to family sharing in financial decisions and adjustments. On this subject 18 freshmen, five seniors, and three alumni commented.

The chief concern of freshmen with regard to control of family finance was the handling of incomes when husband and wife both work. Seniors seemed more interested in the proper allocation of responsibility for the administration of income. Alumni indicated more concern over the self-respect that comes with the financial independence of individual members of the family and the economic responsibility each one bears the other.

FRESHMEN
What should the factor concerning money be if both the wife and husband work? Should the money be controlled jointly, or one or the other have the balance of power?

Who should control the purse string in a family where both husband and wife work?

What is better and works for a more harmonious household, pooling incomes or separate bank accounts?

SENIORS
How should the finances be handled with regard to distribution between husband and wife?

How are we to decide who should take care of home finances, husband or wife?

Cooperation on a business basis between man and wife for domestic harmony.

ALUMNI
Financial responsibility to each other. When and where it ends, to what extent.

Financial control. Our family has always openly discussed all financial problems at all times. I have found this of wonderful value. It teaches one to scrutinize expenditures more closely and to meet their income. Too, it prepares one to step in as head of family at any moment necessary.

I should like to suggest that one of the most important questions which should be discussed among families is that of the economic status of each member. In the light, both of my personal and business experience, I have discovered that the independence of husband and wife, children and parents on a financial basis, contributes to a healthy mutual self-respect, and a harmony among the members, perhaps more than any other factor. Children, who from childhood, are trained to earn their own way, reach adulthood with the ability to stand on their own feet in the competitive world in which we find ourselves. Mothers, who, if unable to spare time from the family to earn their own living, are nevertheless entrusted with their own allowance, need never know the tragedy of a dependent widowhood.

C. Cost of Parenthood

Questions dealing with the cost of parenthood fell into two subgroups: (1) cost of pregnancy, and (2) cost of adequate maintenance of children. Seven freshmen, seven seniors, and two alumni commented.

1. Cost of pregnancy

Occasional questions dealt with the cost of adequate prenatal and postnatal care.

FRESHMAN
How is it possible for those unable to pay for competent medical care during pregnancy to obtain it?

SENIOR
How much does it cost to have the first baby?

ALUMNUS
How much does a baby cost? How can we find the best doctor for the most reasonable price and the best hospital in our own community?

2. *Cost of adequate maintenance of children*

The same concern with the standards of living and economic security of offspring appeared in all groups.

FRESHMEN
Is it advisable to have children if you are without definite financial security?

Should financial problems prevent one from having children until one is able to support them on a high standard of living?

SENIOR
Discussion on number of children advisable under different wage scales and living conditions.

How can a husband and wife live on a certain scale of living and still have children, and how many can they have and still maintain this standard with their income? I believe that we could profit greatly by a knowledge of control of this situation. This is, I believe, the greatest problem, meeting the standards of living and still trying to preserve the family unit.

ALUMNUS
Children: number best for income. How to provide for future.

D. *Savings, Insurance, Investment*

Only three freshmen, three seniors, and eight alumni gave suggestions in this area.

When considering savings, insurance, and investments, seniors and alumni asked for precise information relative to the virtues of investments in stocks and bonds as against bank savings. Freshmen were not interested in the problem of investment of their savings, only in the general problem of saving to meet the exigencies of the so-called "rainy day."

FRESHMEN
Saving for the future?

What is the proper way to spend and yet save enough money to do through "hard times"?

SENIOR

Just what types of insurance are best for a family? Instruction to include life and death insurance, insurance to finance a child's later education, etc.

ALUMNI

Savings and insurance protection of each other. Investments: such as insurance—stocks, if ever—bonds.

Secondly, a good honest course in finances. What banks there are, which to choose for what deposits, how to get the most out of the smallest salary. What insurance agencies to patronize.

E. General Family Finance

The more general questions on family finance were divided into five sub-groups: (1) how to handle family finance, (2) relation of income to standard of living, (3) parent-student finances, (4) importance of money in family life, and (5) financial experience of children and youth. Twenty-nine freshmen, 23 seniors, and 28 alumni gave suggestions that were classified in this division.

1. How to handle family finance

All groups seemed to be interested in problems of family finance. Some of the questions under this heading are rather general in character. However, several have real significance, by implication, in areas other than family economics.

FRESHMAN

How can financial affairs be properly taken care of in the home?

SENIOR

How to establish a sound financial basis for home life. I have found in my own case that finances can crowd most other things out of life, and it is vicious to peace of mind.

ALUMNUS

A course in economics—with theories discarded—and with applications stressed. (All this emphasis on practicality is hardly academic, but what the hell! It takes a few years out of college to give you the conviction that nothing else matters much until you have the leisure and economic security to lapse back into theory.)

2. Relation of income to standard of living

Freshmen, seniors, alumni agreed that achieving a standard of living compatible with one's inner needs and income is a major concern.

FRESHMEN
What standards of living a couple can keep on what salaries.

What are the chances of a successful marriage when only a subsistence wage is earned by the husband?

SENIORS
What income is necessary to support a family to exist, to live, to live luxuriously, in different locations and sections?

Does it make for a happy family if the standard of living is lowered from the one accustomed to when single?

ALUMNI
Type of living to expect: live within income and not push standards too high because of education.

Since I have graduated from college, I have found that the average college man or woman sets his standards of living far too high. If I had not aimed too high in college, I think, perhaps, it could have helped my college life more. It is fine to aim high, but keep your goal within reason.

3. Parent-student finances

The problems of parent-student finances, particularly as they relate to the money invested by parents in college educations for their children, do not always end with the conferring of the degree. While in college the sacrifices made by parents are of grave concern to many students. After graduation, the return to parents of the money invested during college is often a source of worry because of the heavy tax upon their meager earnings and the postponement of marriage.

FRESHMEN
Is it right for a boy or girl to come to college at the extreme sacrifices of the parents? There are a number of students with parents of the laboring classes who are troubled by this problem. I feel this is a mental handicap to the student who never enjoys "College life" (social activities, etc.) because he is struck with the idea that he must labor unceasingly so as not to fail his parents. From still another point of view this gives the boy or girl a sense of obligation to his or her parents. Thus he will not marry unless his parents are "well fixed" financially.

If one or more members of the same family are going to college and if funds are low, should the youngest one be allowed to sacrifice his place so that the older one might finish his course?

Why aren't expenses of college looked upon as the earnings of the student rather than luxury?

SENIOR
Do you think it proper that a college student tax the rather meager resources of parents by asking them to finance him through a rather expensive medical education?

ALUMNUS
One problem in family relations which I think important is economic relations between members of the family. This is especially pertinent just after the student is graduated. After college, there is the necessity of providing for himself and sometimes for others, and paying back the money which he spent to attend college. Women graduates who marry without ever working to support themselves are also faced by the problem of economic relationships in the family.

4. *Importance of money in family life*

The freshman in the following instance takes a somewhat realistic attitude toward a subject of philosophical import. Few suggestions in this sub-group were received.

FRESHMAN
Is it true that when the "bill collector rings at the front door, love goes out the back"? Give three reasons in support of your answer.

SENIOR
What bearing does the economic question have in married life?

ALUMNUS
If possible, they should be taught to be able to satisfy themselves with whatever they have on hand and that the accumulation of a great amount of money is not the most significant thing in life.

5. *Financial experience of children and youth*

Only freshmen and seniors asked questions relative to the problem of financial experience of children and youth. Their interests in this subject seemed to run parallel.

FRESHMAN
Children should know where the family income goes and how much of it is spent on them. It is necessary to have allowances for this. I have mentioned this point because much of the family trouble I have seen has been over money matters.

SENIORS
At what age and to what extent should the financial intricacies of family life be revealed to the child?

Instruction should be given along the line of finances. Many college students should be taught how to handle money for they certainly don't know how.

All students should be taught how to live within their means.

F. Wage-Earning Wife

The problems concerning the wage-earning wife fell into three subgroups: (1) ethics of earning after marriage, (2) factors influencing desirability, and (3) relation of career to success in marriage. On this subject 29 freshmen, 23 seniors, and two alumni commented. The issues involved in a family where the wife assumes responsibilities beyond those of the homemaker aroused considerable comment from freshmen and seniors. Alumni were casual in their reference to the matter or were silent.

1. Ethics of earning after marriage

Occasional concern was demonstrated in the ethics of planning for a woman to work after marriage. With some young people this seemed to be a moral issue.

FRESHMEN
Should the wife be allowed to work if the husband can support the family?
Should the wife be allowed to work if it eases the financial burden of the husband?

SENIORS
Should a woman, if it is not necessary, work after marriage?
Is there any real harm in the wife working at the onset of marriage?

ALUMNI
No comment.

2. Factors influencing desirability

In considering the factors pertaining to the desirability of wage-earning by the wife, the freshmen tended to think in terms of choice while seniors more often considered questions of necessity.

FRESHMAN
Can one have a successful career and marriage?

SENIOR
The problem of the "working wife" is a grave one today and accounts for the lowered birth rate among the middle and upper classes. Some solution

for this need—making it necessary for the wife to be working and contributing to the upkeep of the home during the years when she should be rearing children would result in happier, fuller lives for young people.

ALUMNI
No comment.

3. Relation of career to success in marriage

Comment was received from all groups on this angle of the wage-earning wife's problem. The only alumni responses on the entire area pertained to a successful relationship between career and marriage.

FRESHMAN
What are the chances of combining a career and marriage? Can a woman be successful in both? Will she find enough happiness in a career, such as that of a lawyer or doctor, to give up marriage? Can you give us examples of such women and suggestions?

SENIOR
Should a woman have a career? How do career women make out as mothers and wives?

ALUMNI
Career in addition to housekeeping duties for the wife, or hobbies.

Homemaking possibilities, marriage and careers, etc.

G. Finances Necessary to Marry

Questions concerning finances necessary to marry fell into three sub-groups: (1) minimum income needs for marriage, (2) relation of debts and obligations to marriage plans, (3) importance of money in planning to marry. On this subject 57 freshmen, 26 seniors, and three alumni commented. A very definite similarity of response was provoked by this issue. In most cases it would be difficult to identify the questioner as freshman, senior, or alumni, judging solely by approach and mode of expression.

1. Minimum income needs for marriage

Many young people felt the need for more information on financial resources needed at the beginning of marriage.

FRESHMAN
What is the minimum income that would be necessary for marriage? To support a family?

SENIOR

What the actual minimum costs of married life would be to live happily?

ALUMNUS

What should be regarded as the minimum family income to provide a decent livelihood?

2. *Relation of debts and obligations to marriage plans*

The problem of adjustment between the desire for marriage and the lack of resources troubled both freshmen and seniors.

FRESHMAN

Should a young man who has gone through college on borrowed money delay his marriage until he has repaid the one from whom he received the money? Should he deprive himself of certain things immediately after graduation and make an effort to return the money immediately?

SENIOR

There should be some education along the line of financing early marriages. Men and girls who fall in love during their college days are very often mature enough to enter into the marriage relationship and need it for a normal, wholesome life, but their standards of living have become so high that they are unable to adjust themselves to the sacrifices needed in order to establish a home, and pay college debts.

3. *Importance of money in planning to marry*

The importance of money as a factor for consideration when planning to marry was recognized by all groups as vital.

FRESHMAN

Should two people very decidedly in love refuse to marry because their yearly income is not enough to meet their usual expenditures, but is adequate if they reduce their style of living?

SENIOR

How much should the two parties be earning before marriage takes place?

ALUMNI

The question of finance in determining the date of marriage. Should the economic angle be considered primarily important?

One should be taught to marry only when an income is substantial enough to support a wife and additions to family comfortably.

VIII. CHILDREN

Suggestions dealing with children were classified under the headings: (A) Physical Care, (B) Guidance, (C) Place in the Family, and

(D) Miscellaneous. On these subjects 122 freshmen, 81 seniors, and 40 alumni commented.

A. Physical Care

Suggestions relative to the physical care of children fell into three sub-groups: (1) prenatal care, (2) care and development of babies and children, and (3) health and minor accidents. On this subject 26 freshmen, 14 seniors, and 11 alumni commented. All groups recognized the value of training for young people as potential parents in the prenatal and postnatal care of children. The physical well-being of the child was greatly stressed.

1. Prenatal care

Some concern was expressed with the care of the expectant mother and protection of the child during pregnancy.

FRESHMAN
Care of children, pregnancy, birth, and childhood. Instruction should be given for prenatal care of women.

SENIOR
Various questions of pregnancy.

ALUMNI
Prenatal care and postnatal infant care.

2. Care and development of babies and children

Points of emphasis relative to young children were quite similar in the questions asked by freshmen, seniors, and alumni.

FRESHMAN
I think that one of the most important family matters that should be taken care of in such an instruction course is the care and training of children. Many people of today do not realize the value of knowing how to raise their children.

SENIOR
Instruction should be given on the proper raising of children, especially babies up to 4–6 years.

ALUMNUS
A course in child development from birth through adolescence.

3. Health and minor accidents

The desire to be prepared to protect their children's health extended to a demand for knowledge of first aid and childhood diseases.

FRESHMEN
What are the most prevalent child diseases and what are the best means of, primarily, prevention, and secondly, cure?

Parents should know how to treat minor accidents that occur around the home, such as cut fingers, etc., and antidotes for different poisons that a child might take by accident.

SENIOR
The importance of a knowledge of health in regard to the rearing of children.

ALUMNI
I believe that every young man and woman of marriageable age should be made familiar with the health problems of children and the care of children in emergencies. This is especially important to the young mother.

Health precautions—vaccines and inoculations preventing contagion.

B. Guidance

Questions dealing with some aspect of guidance of children fell into four sub-groups: (1) rearing and guidance of children, (2) child psychology, (3) discipline, and (4) allocation of responsibility for guidance. On this subject 54 freshmen, 42 seniors, and 27 alumni commented. All groups seemed to realize the value of training for parents in this field.

1. Rearing and guidance of children

Questions on child guidance were seldom clear cut although many young people were aware of problems in this area.

FRESHMAN
My parents and others have told of mistakes they have made in raising their children and realized these mistakes only too late. I would eagerly elect in my course some subject pertaining to the development of the intellect and character of children from the very beginning of their lives.

SENIORS
Particular stress, I believe, should be placed upon the rearing of children to prepare them for better living in society and the fulfillment of *their own* lives to the greatest satisfaction of themselves, their parents, and society in general.

How to manage and bring up a family to be respectable citizens?

ALUMNUS
Prospective parents and members of families must learn that it is important to teach their children a good set of values, starting at a quite early age.

For example, children must realize early that money, power, and position have too long been overemphasized, and that such traits as ability to live harmoniously with other people, ability to compromise, tolerance, appreciation of such things as music, books, and beauty in general are far more important.

2. *Child psychology*

All groups, freshmen, seniors, and alumni, appeared to place a high value upon training in child psychology in order that they, as parents, might help their children to develop to the fullness of their powers, and that the parent-child relationship might be mutually rich and satisfying.

FRESHMAN
Psychology of raising children so as to make it possible for them to have the greatest happiness in their life.

SENIOR
Something concerning the care and training of children, not only physical care, but mental and emotional as well.

ALUMNI
General course in the elements of psychoanalytic principles and their application from a normal point of view. This should include personality development from birth, with emphasis on the positive factors going to create a well-balanced individual with constructively and healthfully directed drives for living.

A practical course in child psychology.

Purpose: to help those intending to rear families, or be members of families having children, to be mentally and emotionally equipped to handle children to their mutual advantage.

3. *Discipline*

The subject of direct discipline brought forth only three comments, two from freshmen—the group more vitally concerned with the problems of self-assertion, and one from a senior.

FRESHMEN
Just what attitudes or relationships should be maintained between parents and children on the problem of discipline?

Most important of all, some instructions as to the best way of raising children—whether it is better to "spare the rod and spoil the child."

SENIOR
Various methods of discipline for children. How to deal with different types of personalities in children (problem children).

4. *Allocation of responsibility for guidance*

The problem of divided parental responsibility for the training of a child was the concern only of undergraduates.

FRESHMEN
How should the task of rearing the children be divided?
A course on rearing children should be given to both sexes. Probably the men wouldn't need to know quite as much about this as the women should. They should be given a good, stiff course in this.

SENIORS
What relationship should the parents have to the child? Just what part is the mother's part? What is the father's part?
How can it be settled so that husband and wife share alike in the raising of children?

ALUMNI
No comment.

C. *Place of Children in the Family*

The place of the child in the family was approached from two angles: (1) when to have children, and (2) role of the child in the family. On this subject, 40 freshmen, 20 seniors, and two alumni commented.

1. *When to have children*

The spacing of children in relation to family values appeared to interest undergraduate students.

FRESHMEN
How many children can the average woman have in the average home without destroying her vitality and the savings of the family?
Is it wise to have one's children in the first years of marriage?

SENIOR
How to govern, when couple should have a child—income, physical status, mental attitudes?

ALUMNUS
Most young couples face immediately after marriage the problem of children. How soon should we have one? How much do parents owe children and vice versa?

2. *Role of the child in the family*

The relation a child bears to the quality of family life was of interest to all groups, particularly freshmen.

FRESHMEN
Is there a tendency for childless married couples to break up more easily than married couples having children?

Is it possible to have a modern, successful marriage without having a child for a "binding" influence?

Can two married people live a full and happy life without children?

SENIOR
Influence of presence of children in home on happiness in married life.

ALUMNUS
Children in marriage; childless marriage.

D. Miscellaneous

Only two freshmen and five seniors gave suggestions that were classified under this heading. They pertained to the education of children, adoption, and parentless children. Freshman comments were indefinite but those from seniors were fairly specific.

FRESHMEN
Education in the home.

Education of the children.

SENIORS
Private versus public schools for children.

How to provide for the future education of your children.

What hazards in child training does an unmarried woman take when she adopts foundlings? Is such a home fair to the children?

Adoption—how to go about it. Should the child be told?

Homes for parentless children and children for childless parents.

ALUMNI
No comment.

IX. RELIGION AND ETHICS

Suggestions dealing with religion and ethics were classified under two headings: (A) Parent-Child Religious Problems, and (B) Function in Family Life. On these subjects 26 freshmen, 10 seniors, and 18 alumni expressed themselves.

A. Parent-Child Religious Problems

This was primarily a freshman interest having to do with the allocation of responsibility for deciding the child's religious affiliation. Except for two questions dealing with church attendance and choice (both given below), the questions all hinged on the difficulties arising because of difference in religious beliefs of parents. In all, 10 freshmen and three seniors commented.

FRESHMEN

Do you think it is a good thing for a child to have too much to say in respect to its choice of a religion?

How to avoid complications of differences in religious beliefs in raising children?

After marriage should the husband go with the wife to her church or vice versa? Or should this problem be decided upon before marriage? Where should the children go if each goes to a different church?

SENIORS

Should a child be made to go to church? How could it be arranged that a child could decide for himself which church, if any, he wanted to attend?

Should religious difference between parents influence the training of the child? That is, should there be any greater lack of harmony because of differing religious background than because of different national background?

The question of religion. How to bridge the gap between the ideas of parents and the ever lessening desire of children for a great tie-up with religion.

B. Function in Family Life

Suggestions dealing with the function of religion and ethics in family life fell into two sub-groups: (1) role of religion in family life, and (2) general ethical behavior and values. Sixteen freshmen, seven seniors, and 18 alumni commented in this area.

1. Role of religion in family life

All groups revealed interest in the role religion may play in family life.

FRESHMEN

What is the part of religion in family life and marriage?

What should be the religious participation of the family as a unit?

Can a marriage be really successful without a spiritual background? How important is similarity of spiritual background, i. e., Catholic vs. Protestant?

SENIORS

Should the question of religion be given much emphasis?

Religion—one for the family today—one that will fit and serve its purpose.

ALUMNI
Religion in marriage.

An adequate Christian background. One who is in constant communion with God will not go far wrong in family life.

2. *General ethical behavior and values*

Reference to ethical values was made by freshmen, seniors, and alumni but the comments were few (four in all) and somewhat vague.

X. MISCELLANEOUS

In this category were assembled a varied group of comments and suggestions. Some represented forceful thinking but were not sufficiently representative of the group as a whole to warrant analysis. A few were too vague and confused in meaning to be classified elsewhere.

The suggestions in the Miscellaneous category were grouped under the headings: (A) Techniques of Homemaking, (B) Social Behavior, (C) Vocations, and (D) Unclassified. They included 66 items suggested by freshmen, 46 by seniors, and 95 by alumni.

A. Techniques of Homemaking

In this sub-group the questions and suggestions stress the need for practical knowledge in home management, and for technical skills and information.

FRESHMEN
Teach women to cook a substantial meal.

Organization of a well-balanced home.

Stress cleanliness of body and surroundings.

SENIORS
Practical nursing instruction should be part of all women's curriculum.

Is it necessary that the wife know how to cook? What are the financial problems that arise when she doesn't?

ALUMNI
What is important for the building of a permanent relationship is a thorough knowledge of practical economics. This can be done in two ways. If the male side of the population would raise the standard of demands upon the accomplishments of the women, one would soon see that girls would know how to buy good fruit and vegetables, how to select ma-

terials for draperies and durable rugs, why this store has the best buy, when to plant certain flowers, what to do in case of emergencies, what is expected of one who manages a home. The second which works hand in hand with the first would be to have students required to take courses along these lines to make them conscious of the necessity of this knowledge.

The young woman should have an elementary but workable idea on how to manage a household. All girls cannot learn to be domestic science experts, but they should have some idea of the problems confronting the average housewife.

B. Social Behavior

Freshmen, seniors, and alumni expressed a desire for training in the amenities of living. It is interesting to note that recognition of the value of such knowledge tended to increase with the age and experience of the subject. Five freshmen, nine seniors, and 15 alumni gave suggestions that ranged from a demand for training in the most elementary techniques of etiquette to a consideration of hobbies as a means of developing social grace and personal poise.

FRESHMEN

Refinement should be taught in college as well as any other studies for there are some pupils who never learn this at home.

I believe the most important thing is manners. Good manners should be taught so that young people feel they can marry some one in their own social class.

SENIORS

How to act in company and good manners.

Colleges would do well to have compulsory courses for all students in etiquette. When you don't have to be ashamed of your partner's social conduct, when you have nothing to reproach each other for after an evening in society, friction is greatly lessened.

Social behavior. A thorough course in this work should be compulsory. So many of us are not at ease at the table or when in the company of a stranger because we are not certain about the proper way to act. I am very much in favor of a detailed course in social behavior, which to me is a very essential factor toward making one a happier person.

ALUMNI

The art of being gracious.

Students need help in the adjustments necessary between persons, groups, and so on. They need help in matters of common courtesy and etiquette.

Perhaps a point or two could be taken from the "finishing school" as far as the social amenities are concerned for both men and women—including something of both private and social etiquette, dancing, bridge playing, tennis, golf, anything else that promotes better companionship between wife and husband, or with other groups. I think most college graduates would be a lot better off if they could dance adequately, play a fair game of bridge, introduce some one properly, or swim a hundred yards.

C. *Vocations*

The interest in vocations reflected the period of economic unrest during which the participants in this study were attending college or entering a field of professional competition. On this subject seven freshmen, eight seniors, and 13 alumni suggested items. Members of each group voiced bitter thinking about unemployment.

FRESHMAN
What should a college graduate do when he cannot get a job? What good is education if a college graduate cannot make any use of it? Of what use is a college education to a man today?

SENIOR
Why go to college when we can't get jobs when we get out?

ALUMNUS
What remedy would be beneficial to get around an out-of-job psychosis?

All groups recognized the importance of deliberation before selecting a vocation.

FRESHMAN
I believe the hardest thing for any person is finding out what you are best suited for. Many young men and women attend school and pick courses in which they are misfits. Many start college not knowing what vocation or profession they intend to follow. If there were only some way in which to find the vocation, profession, or business that we are fitted for, it would save much time, money, and anxiety.

SENIOR
Better guidance should be given so that the student knows what to expect upon leaving school; i. e., the practical side to the vocation or profession should be easily available.

ALUMNI
Occupation: think hard before you make your choice.

I believe more attention should be given to providing students some information regarding the chance in their chosen field, that is, a little knowledge of the supply and demand. Too many undergraduates choose a profession for unwise reasons: they think it sounds grand to be a doctor; they have a favorite uncle who is a lawyer; it is easy to prepare for teaching. They don't know anything about the abilities required in certain jobs and it might help a great deal if they did.

D. *Unclassified*

Under the heading "Unclassified" fell a diversity of suggestions, 22 items from freshmen, nine from seniors, and 50 from alumni. The category included such vague suggestions as these asked by freshmen:

"Are you happy with your present mode of living?"

"Is there such a thing as a formula for life?"

Many of the alumni suggestions classified in the sub-group were extremely pertinent to the problems of living today, but the particularized items were too limited in number and too scattered in content to warrant separate sub-groupings.

ALUMNI

Enable the student to retain individuality and faith in himself and his ideals after being "dumped" into the masses.

One must be a good citizen and play straight with the government and his employer.

I wish that my course had allowed time for special project work in the community, not merely book knowledge.

I sincerely wish that college had trained me to be an intelligent voter. To cover all courses on federal, state, county, and municipal government means to major in Political Science. That is not every student's desire. Yet to have earned a degree should mean that I, for one, can vote intelligently with a definite responsibility.

SUMMARY

A total of 2,752 suggestions concerning instruction on marriage and the family were received from 632 students and alumni participating in the study. The number of suggestions per person ranged from one to 16, with a median of 4.4. Eighty-seven per cent of the participants gave more than one suggestion. Usually those made by one person dealt with several aspects of preparation for marriage and family living.

With few exceptions the items suggested were clearly expressed and relevant to the problem. The responses of both undergraduate students and alumni seemed to be frank, sincere, and free from jest. There was no evidence of deliberate effort to conceal or distort. The responses of many participants tended to form patterns reflecting clearly some of their immediate personal problems.

5:
Analysis of Suggestions Given by Groups of Participants

W_IDELY varied interests in certain areas of instruction in marriage and family living were revealed by the responses of different groups. The number and type of suggestions offered were assumed to disclose areas of greater and lesser concern. In several categories men and women differed in the number of items submitted. Freshmen, seniors, and alumni differed in areas of emphasis, an area important to one being relatively unimportant to another. Certainly this diversity of emphasis and its association with college, maturity, sex, and other traits of student and alumni groups have direct implications in planning programs for youth.

DIFFERENCES IN VOLUME OF RESPONSE AMONG PARTICIPANTS

As stated previously, 2,752 separate suggestions were written on the free response forms. The distribution of these items among categories for each college, class, and sex is summarized in Table 4. The number of suggestions per person varied little from college to college. Participants from "S" suggested 1,803 items, or 4.4 per person, as contrasted with 949 items, or an average of 4.2 per person, by participants from "T." Although freshmen and seniors were given only 20 minutes in which to respond, whereas alumni had unlimited time, freshmen suggested an average of 4.0 items per person, seniors 5.4 items per person, and alumni 3.9 items per person. The mean number of items suggested by seniors was sufficiently large in relation to the means for other classes to indicate that a real difference existed between the volume of response from seniors and either freshmen or alumni. It is

TABLE 4. *Distribution Among Categories of 2,752 Items Pertaining to Instruction in Marriage and Family Life by 632 Participants*

COLLEGE, CLASS, AND SEX	I	II	III	IV	V	VI	VII	VIII	IX	X	TOTAL NUMBER OF ITEMS
"T" freshman men.....	3	22	66	62	26	12	33	25	9	26	284
"T" freshman women..		19	13	10	11	6	8	4	1	6	78
"S" freshman men.....	7	35	172	175	63	19	97	73	12	24	677
"S" freshman women...		20	65	51	31	11	39	20	4	10	251
All freshmen........	10	96	316	298	131	48	177	122	26	66	1,290
"T" senior men........	5	9	40	67	40	12	26	19	3	11	232
"T" senior women.....	2	17	26	54	24	6	26	19		3	177
"S" senior men........	7	14	62	75	39	15	36	26	4	18	296
"S" senior women.....	4	12	36	33	28	12	27	17	3	14	186
All seniors..........	18	52	164	229	131	45	115	81	10	46	891
"T" alumni..........	4	2	4	31	16	2	7	6	5	18	95
"T" alumnae..........	1	3	6	19	21	2	9	7	1	14	83
"S" alumni..........	3	9	15	59	48	4	38	16	5	47	244
"S" alumnae..........	4	3	11	29	39	4	25	11	7	16	149
All alumni..........	12	17	36	138	124	12	79	40	18	95	571
All "T" participants...	15	72	155	243	138	40	109	80	19	78	949
All "S" participants....	25	93	361	422	248	65	262	163	35	129	1,803
All "T" and "S" men...	29	91	359	469	232	64	237	165	38	144	1,828
All "T" and "S" women	11	74	157	196	154	41	134	78	16	63	924
All participants........	40	165	516	665	386	105	371	243	54	207	2,752

interesting to recall (see page 16) that many college courses on the family are open only to upperclassmen and that courses are more frequently offered by colleges where women are enrolled than in men's colleges. Women contributed a significantly larger number of items than men. Men gave 4.1 suggestions per person as contrasted with 4.9 items, the mean for women. The ratios of the mean difference to the standard deviation of the mean difference for the groups compared were as follows: "T" and "S," 0.91; men and women, 3.56; freshmen and seniors, 5.33; seniors and alumni, 4.94.

DISTRIBUTION OF FREE RESPONSE ITEMS
AMONG CATEGORIES

The distribution of suggestions among categories was believed to give some indication of the extent of undergraduate and alumni concern within given areas. The percentage distribution of the 2,752 items among categories appears in Table 5. Considering the distribution of the total group of responses without reference to college, class, or sex, the category in which the largest number of items appeared was Category IV—Sex, which included 665 items or 24 per cent of the total number of suggestions given. In rank order from greatest to smallest frequency of items the categories were:

(1) Category IV—Sex, with 665 items or 24.2 per cent of the total.
(2) Category III—Premarriage Problems, with 516 items or 18.8 per cent of the total.
(3) Category V—Accord, with 386 items or 14.0 per cent of the total.
(4) Category VII—Family Economics, with 371 items or 13.5 per cent of the total.
(5) Category VIII—Children, with 243 items or 8.8 per cent of the total.
(6) Category X—Miscellaneous, with 207 items or 7.5 per cent of the total.
(7) Category II—Two and Three Generation Adjustments, with 165 items or 6.0 per cent of the total.
(8) Category VI—Discord, with 105 items or 3.8 per cent of the total.
(9) Category IX—Religion and Ethics, with 54 items or 2.0 per cent of the total.
(10) Category I—The Family as a Social Institution, with 40 items or 1.4 per cent of the total.

Seniors and alumni suggested more items in Category IV—Sex than in any other area, and this category received the second largest number of all items suggested by freshmen. The fact that all freshmen had received recently some instruction concerning the anatomy and

TABLE 5. *Number and Percentage Distribution Among Categories of 2,752 Items Pertaining to Instruction in Marriage and Family Life, Suggested by 320 Freshmen, 164 Seniors, and 148 Alumni, Evaluated in Terms of the Differences in Percentage Between Given Classes*

CATEGORY	FRESHMEN		SENIORS		ALUMNI		ALL PARTICIPANTS		DIFF. IN %/σ DIFF.	
	Number	Per Cent	Number	Per Cent	Number	Per Cent	Number	Per Cent	Freshmen and Seniors	Seniors and Alumni
I. Family as a Social Institution............	10	0.8%	18	2.0%	12	2.1%	40	1.4%	−3.5	−0.1
II. Two and Three Generation Adjustments......	96	7.4	52	5.8	17	3.0	165	6.0	+1.8	+2.4
III. Premarriage Problems..	316	24.5	164	18.4	36	6.3	516	18.8	+4.1	+6.5
IV. Sex......................	298	23.1	229	25.7	138	24.2	665	24.2	−1.7	+0.7
V. Accord...................	131	10.2	131	14.7	124	21.7	386	14.0	−3.9	−3.5
VI. Discord.................	48	3.7	45	5.0	12	2.1	105	3.8	−1.9	+2.8
VII. Family Economics......	177	13.7	115	12.9	79	13.8	371	13.5	+0.7	−0.5
VIII. Children.............	122	9.5	81	9.1	40	7.0	243	8.8	+0.4	+1.4
IX. Religion and Ethics....	26	2.0	10	1.1	18	3.2	54	2.0	+1.8	−2.7
X. Miscellaneous...........	66	5.1	46	5.2	95	16.6	207	7.5	−0.1	−7.1
All categories.............	1,290		891		571		2,752	100.0%		

physiology of sex in required physical education and hygiene courses may have influenced this response. The function of this instruction in answering questions and resolving or increasing perplexities was not explored. Table 5 shows that the largest number of items suggested by freshmen in any one category, 24.5 per cent, was in Category III— Premarriage Problems. However, Category IV—Sex ranked a close second for it received 23 per cent. Seniors gave Category III the second largest number of items; Category V ranked second in order of frequency of suggestions by alumni. It will be recalled that Category III includes items dealing with courtship adjustments, when and whom to marry, topics assumed to be of great interest to seniors, the group with the largest number of persons engaged to be married.

Freshmen and alumni, as well as the group as a whole, suggested the smallest number of items in Category I—The Family as a Social Institution. Less than 1 per cent of the total number of items suggested by freshmen and only 2 per cent suggested by alumni were classified in this category. The request was in a form which emphasized guidance in personal problems in order to contribute "to more satisfying family life now and to more successful marriage" and could not be expected to stimulate many responses dealing with the history of the family or the family as a social institution. However, it is interesting to observe that the two groups which gave fewest suggestions in this area reported widely different amounts of college instruction in sociology which might, presumably, deal with the family as a social institution. Whereas fewer than one in 10 freshmen reported having had a college course in sociology, three out of four alumni stated completion of one or more courses in this field. Of the three groups, seniors suggested the fewest items in Category IX—Religion and Ethics. Significant differences in the distribution of items among given areas by freshmen and seniors were found in only three out of 10 categories. Between seniors and alumni, the distributions varied significantly in five out of 10 categories.

NUMBER OF PERSONS SUGGESTING ITEMS IN EACH CATEGORY

The number of persons expressing interest in a given area may be a more valid index of concern than the volume of response. Since some

TABLE 6. *Number of Free Response Items and Number of Persons Responding in Given Categories Suggested by 320 Freshmen, 164 Seniors, and 148 Alumni*

CATEGORY	FRESHMEN		SENIORS		ALUMNI	
	Persons	Items	Persons	Items	Persons	Items
I. Family as a Social Institution......	10	10	17	18	12	12
II. Two and Three Generation Adjustments..........	65	96	37	52	11	17
III. Premarriage Problems....	180	316	86	164	30	36
IV. Sex.....................	185	298	121	229	92	138
V. Accord.................	102	131	84	131	75	124
VI. Discord.................	42	48	38	45	9	12
VII. Family Economics.......	136	177	77	115	64	79
VIII. Children...............	96	122	65	81	35	40
IX. Religion and Ethics.......	24	26	9	10	17	18
X. Miscellaneous..........	46	66	34	46	64	95

persons gave more than one item per category, the data were analyzed to determine the number of individuals giving suggestions in each area, regardless of the number of items. Table 6 shows more persons suggested items in Category IV—Sex than in any other category. Of 632 participants, 398 persons or 62.8 per cent of the total group suggested items dealing with sex information or sex adjustment. Proposals in this category not only represent approximately one out of every four items but include suggestions made by more than three out of every five participants. As could be anticipated from a group of young unmarried men and women, the second largest number of persons, 296 or 46.8 per cent of the total group, suggested items dealing with premarriage problems. These were classified in Category III—Premarriage Problems.

Items classified in Category VII—Family Economics were received from 277 persons or 43.7 per cent of all participants. Items classified in Category V—Accord were suggested by 261 persons or 40.8 per cent of all participants. In contrast with accord (the positive approach to family adjustments), discord (the negative approach) received relatively little emphasis. Only 14.0 per cent of all participants suggested items in Category VI—Discord. Apparently many more subjects were concerned with prophylaxis rather than cure with regard to family relationship. Slightly fewer than one third of all participants suggested items in Category VIII—Children. Items in Category II—Two and Three Generation Adjustments were suggested by 17.9 per cent of all participants. Fewer than one person in 10 suggested items in Category IX—Religion and Ethics, or in Category I—The Family as a Social Institution.

The relative emphasis among categories in terms of rank order of both volume of response and number of persons responding was substantially the same. Category IV—Sex received the largest proportion of all items contributed by the largest number of participants. Category I—The Family as a Social Institution received the smallest number of items and had the smallest number of contributing participants.

DISTRIBUTION OF FREE RESPONSE ITEMS AND COLLEGE

The questions and suggestions given by "T" and "S" participants differed somewhat in distribution among categories. The distribution of all "T" and "S" suggestions is summarized among the last five lines of Table 4 on page 108. When interpreting these data it should be recalled that approximately two out of three persons were from "S" college.

The chi-square technique was used to test the hypothesis that there was no association between the frequency of free response items per category and college. The results of the test appear in Table 7. Since the chi-square obtained was somewhat larger than the tabled chi-square for the corresponding number of degrees of freedom at the $F_{.01}$ level of probability, the hypothesis was rejected. The differences in distribution of items by "T" and "S" participants were sufficiently large to suggest that there probably was a real difference between groups.

The greatest differences appeared in Category II—Two and Three Generation Adjustments and Category X—Miscellaneous, where "T" participants gave a slightly larger response than "S," and in Category III—Premarriage Problems and VII—Family Economics, where, "S" participants gave a slightly larger response. The greater concern of

TABLE 7. *Association of Distribution Among Categories of Free Response Items with Other Factors*

Factor Tested for Association with Distribution of Items	Chi-Square Obtained	Degrees of Freedom	Probability
College			
"T" and "S" freshmen..........	33.91	9	<.01
"T" and "S" seniors............	14.50	9	.10–.20
"T" and "S" alumni..........	6.69	9	.50–.70
All "T" and "S" participants..	55.10 *	27	<.01
College class			
"T" freshmen and seniors.......	37.49	9	<.01
"T" seniors and alumni.........	60.56	9	<.01
"S" freshmen and seniors........	26.76	9	<.01
"S" seniors and alumni.........	71.55	9	<.01
All "T" and "S" participants..	228.50	18	<.01
Sex			
"T" freshman men and women...	23.37	9	<.01
"S" freshman men and women...	11.94	9	.20–.30
All freshman men and women....	27.42	9	<.01
All senior men and women......	9.21	9	.30–.50
All alumni men and women.....	10.18	9	.30–.50
All men and women..........	46.81	27	<.01
Marital state			
Single and engaged alumni......	12.71	9	.10–.20
Engaged and married alumni.....	7.41	9	.50–.70
Single, engaged, and married undergraduates....................	45.14	18	<.01
Single, engaged, and married alumni......................	23.36	18	< 01
All single, engaged, and married participants................	48.90	18	<.01
Rating of family life (in terms of ideal, successful and satisfactory, and less than satisfactory)			
Freshman ratings...............	49.78	18	<.01
Senior ratings..................	20.86	18	.20–.30
Alumni ratings.................	23.95	18	.10–.20
All ratings....................	94.59 *	54	<.01
Parents			
Parents together and separated or divorced....................	12.78	18	.10–.20

* Additive chi-square.

"T" students and alumni with parent-youth adjustments may be associated with the fact that more "T" than "S" participants lived with relatives. Freedom from family supervision in association with the other sex and in the use of money may have some bearing on the fact that young people from "S" gave a somewhat larger number of suggestions on dating and money management than young people from "T."

When the distributions of free response items written by "T" and "S" participants were compared in sub-groups divided according to class, it was apparent that greatest variation occurred between "T" and "S" freshmen. The chi-square obtained indicated that these freshman groups differed significantly in distribution of items among categories. However, the chi-squares obtained using data for seniors and alumni from "T" and "S" indicated that there is no association between the distribution of free response items and college among groups. It is evident that seniors and alumni from the two colleges were more homogeneous with respect to the distribution of free response items per category than were freshmen. This was also true of the subjects from "T" and "S" colleges with regard to background traits.

DISTRIBUTION OF FREE RESPONSE ITEMS AND COLLEGE CLASS

The suggestions received from freshmen, seniors, and alumni, irrespective of college, differed somewhat in distribution among categories, as shown in Table 5 on page 110. Freshmen suggested a larger proportion of all items in Category III—Premarriage Problems than seniors. Freshmen were younger than seniors and were in process of working out new relationships with both parents and contemporaries. Being in college meant for many changing status in the family group with greater demands by the young people for freedom of action and with more recognition by parents of increasing maturity in decisions on dating. The freedom of association of boys and girls in coeducational colleges may be associated with the relatively large number of questions received from freshmen concerning youth relationships, and whom and when to marry. Freshmen suggested a smaller proportion of all items in Categories V—Accord and I—The Family as a Social Institution than seniors.

The large number of senior items in Category V may be related to the fact that many more seniors than freshmen were engaged to be married. Plans for marriage may have directed more attention to questions and suggestions dealing with family relationships. Also, the fact that a significantly larger number of seniors than freshmen had taken courses in sociology may have been a factor in the apparent greater concern of seniors with the role of the institution of the family in society today. Only these three categories revealed differences greater than could be expected in samples from a population in which there was no real difference.* However, the findings of the Chi-Square Test, summarized in Table 7, indicate that the total distribution of items suggested by freshmen varied from the total distribution of items by seniors to a degree that indicates distributions of items and class were associated.

The distributions of free response items suggested by seniors and by alumni appeared to vary more than the distributions of items by freshmen and seniors. There is no reason to believe that the total distributions by seniors and alumni are associated. Statistical analysis of the significance of the difference in percentage of total response in each category indicated that the differences between senior and alumni responses in four categories were large enough to be considered real. Seniors gave a significantly larger proportion of all items in Category III—Premarriage Problems. This is not unreasonable in view of the fact that more alumni than seniors were married. Probably even the unmarried alumni who were employed had less intimate day-to-day contacts with young men and women than when they were college students. Questions and suggestions dealing with choice of a mate represented more than half of all senior items in Category III. Seniors also suggested a larger number of items in Category VI—Discord than did alumni. Whether the greater emphasis placed on discord by seniors indicates more objective analysis and awareness of discord in the parental home, more concern with avoiding discord in their prospective marriages, or more recent study of divorce and family disintegration in sociology courses is not known.

Alumni suggested a significantly larger proportion of items than seniors in Categories X—Miscellaneous, V—Accord, and IX—Religion

* See the last two columns in Table 5 on page 110.

and Ethics. Many of the alumni items in Category X dealt with vocations and with social and economic conditions facing students after graduation. A larger proportion of all items in Category V—Accord concerned with the psychology of adjustment, leisure interest, and general family relations were suggested by alumni than by seniors. Alumni suggested more items on the function of religion in family living than seniors. These were classified in Category IX—Religion and Ethics. Although the difference in the proportion of total senior and alumni items classified in Category II—Two and Three Generation Adjustments is of doubtful significance, it was evident that seniors suggested more items than alumni dealing with adjustments to relatives after marriage. Many items indicated concern with "in-law" problems. As judged by distribution of suggestions, seniors and alumni differed significantly in the relative emphasis placed in five of the 10 categories, whereas freshmen and seniors differed significantly on only three.

NUMBER OF ITEMS PER PERSON IN EACH CATEGORY

One index of acuteness of concern may be the number of items each individual suggested in a given area. For this reason the variation between the distribution of items among categories was analyzed in terms of the number of items per person as well as in terms of the total number of items per class. The distribution among categories of the number of items per person appears in Table 6 on page 112. Freshmen and seniors differed significantly with respect to the number of items suggested in Category V—Accord. Seniors suggested a larger number of items per person dealing with accord in family adjustment than freshmen. However, the difference between the number of items per person in this area suggested by seniors and by alumni was of questionable significance, although alumni, more of whom were married, tended to suggest a larger number of items per person in Category V—Accord than seniors.

With respect to the number of responses per person per category in Category III—Premarriage Problems, the variation between under-graduates and alumni considered as groups was significantly greater than the variations among individuals within those groups. The difference between undergraduates and alumni in the number of responses per person is in harmony with the significant differences found in percentage distribution of items between freshmen and seniors and between seniors and alumni.

To summarize these findings, the total distribution of free response items suggested by freshmen, seniors, and alumni varied to a degree that makes it reasonable to accept the hypothesis that college class and distribution of items were associated. Significant differences were found between freshmen and seniors and between seniors and alumni in the distribution of items and the number of items per person in Category III—Premarriage Problems and Category V—Accord. Significant differences were found between freshmen and seniors in the distribution of items in Category I—The Family as a Social Institution, and between seniors and alumni in the distribution of items in Categories VI—Discord, IX—Religion and Ethics, and X—Miscellaneous.

DISTRIBUTION OF FREE RESPONSE ITEMS AND SEX OF PARTICIPANT

Since instruction in marriage and family living frequently is given in segregated classes, the association between sex and areas was explored. Senior men and women and alumni men and women varied little with respect to the distribution of items suggested on the free response forms. Although the differences are not significant, there was a general trend for men to suggest a larger number of items than women in Category IV—Sex. A recent study reports that college students rank sex as an area in which they have the liveliest interest, with men indicating more active interest than women [25]. Undergraduate women tended to suggest a somewhat larger number of items than men in Category II—Two and Three Generation Adjustments. However, it is questionable whether distribution of free response items and sex are associated for the group as a whole.

The results of the Chi-Square Test indicate that the hypothesis can be accepted that there is no association between distribution of items among categories and sex with respect to both senior and alumni men and women. Ten freshman men but not one freshman woman suggested items dealing with the family as a social institution. Freshman women suggested a larger proportion of items than freshman men in Categories II—Two and Three Generation Adjustment, V—Accord, and VI—Discord. Results of tests of association appear in Table 7, on page 114. Except for freshmen, men and women participating in the study varied so little in distribution of free response items among categories that the hypothesis was accepted that there is no association between frequency of items per category and sex.

DISTRIBUTION OF FREE RESPONSE ITEMS AND MARITAL STATUS

Marital status and frequency of free response items per category appear to be associated. Persons who were married tended to give a larger proportion of items in Category VII—Family Economics than those who were not married. (See Table 8.) Participants who were engaged to be married tended to give a larger proportion of items in Categories VII—Family Economics and X—Miscellaneous than those who were not engaged to be married. The unmarried undergraduate students who were not engaged tended to suggest a larger percentage of total items in Category III—Premarriage Problems than those who were married or engaged. When the Chi-Square Test was administered it indicated that it is reasonable to reject the hypothesis that there is no association beween frequency of free response items per category and marital status.

When the association between distribution of items and marital status of alumni was analyzed in greater detail, it was found that the differences in the total distribution of items between married and engaged alumni were so small that they might readily have been due to sampling variation rather than to real differences in the population. The small chi-square obtained in testing the hypothesis that there is no association between the frequency of items per category for engaged and not engaged alumni leads to acceptance of the hypothesis. The distributions of items by married and engaged alumni, excluding the single who are not engaged, do not vary significantly. The number of undergraduates who were married was too small to justify similar comparisons among freshmen and seniors.

TABLE 8. *Distribution Among Categories of 2,752 Free Response Items Suggested by 484 Undergraduate and 148 Alumni Participants Classified According to Marital Status*

CATEGORY	UNDERGRADUATES			ALUMNI		
	Married	Engaged	Single	Married	Engaged	Single
I. Family as a Social Institution		3	25	2		10
II. Two and Three Generation Adjustments	1	11	136	5	4	8
III. Premarriage Problems		20	460	9	6	21
IV. Sex	1	51	475	30	12	96
V. Accord	1	25	236	30	11	83
VI. Discord		7	86	7	2	3
VII. Family Economics	1	31	260	25	6	48
VIII. Children		16	187	8	4	28
IX. Religion and Ethics	1	2	33	6	1	11
X. Miscellaneous		6	106	18	13	64
All Items	5	172	2,004	140	59	372

DISTRIBUTION OF FREE RESPONSE ITEMS AND RATING OF FAMILY LIFE

The distribution of items and the ratings assigned present family life appear to be associated if the total group of participants is considered. When the group is divided into three parts according to college class, the hypothesis that there is no association between the distribution of items and rating of family life can be rejected with respect to freshmen only. With respect to seniors and alumni, the results of the Chi-Square Test listed in Table 7 (page 114) indicate that it is reasonable to accept the null hypothesis. Freshmen who rated family life indifferent or still less satisfactory gave a larger percentage of total response in Categories II—Two and Three Generation Adjustments, and V—Accord than freshmen who rated family life satisfactory or better. This suggests that those dissatisfied with their family life

TABLE 9. *Distribution Among Categories of Free Response Items Suggested by Participants Grouped According to Class and Rating Assigned to Present Family Life*

PARTICIPANTS CLASSIFIED ACCORDING TO CLASS AND RATING OF FAMILY LIFE	NUMBER OF FREE RESPONSE ITEMS PER CATEGORY									
	I	II	III	IV	V	VI	VII	VIII	IX	X
Freshmen										
Ideal rating............	1	20	82	63	18	8	31	28	7	14
Successful and satisfactory	9	50	208	205	91	34	129	81	12	44
Indifferent and less favorable................		27	26	29	22	6	17	13	6	6
Seniors										
Ideal rating............	2	3	26	43	19	10	19	7	4	6
Successful and satisfactory	14	37	120	160	96	31	81	64	4	35
Indifferent and less favorable................	2	12	18	25	16	4	14	10	2	4
Alumni										
Ideal rating............	1		1	8	16		7	7	3	5
Successful and satisfactory	7	11	16	68	60	3	36	20	5	56
Indifferent and less favorable................	2	1	9	30	17	1	10	5	3	15

may be experiencing conflict with parents and that they may have a special interest in achieving harmony. The distribution by groups who rated their family life differently appears in Table 9.

Only six of the 39 participants whose parents were separated or divorced suggested items in Category VI—Discord. All were freshmen, one of whom suggested two items. On the other hand, 61 undergraduate students whose parents lived together suggested 72 items in this same area.

The analysis of variance technique applied to these data resulted in an obtained F considerably smaller than the tabled $F_{.01}$ for the corresponding numbers of degrees of freedom. These findings presented in Table 11 (page 123) indicate that there is no significant difference in the number of items suggested in Category VI—Discord between groups from broken and from unbroken homes. The Chi-Square Test was applied to data pertaining to the distribution of items given by all persons whose parents were separated or divorced and by all whose

TABLE 10. *Distribution Among Categories of Free Response Items Suggested by Participants Reporting Parents Together, Separated, or Divorced*

| | NUMBER OF FREE RESPONSE ITEMS SUGGESTED BY PARTICIPANTS | |
CATEGORY	Parents Separated or Divorced	Parents Together
I. Family as a Social Institution.........	1	39
II. Two and Three Generation Adjustments	4	161
III. Premarriage Problems................	11	505
IV. Sex.................................	12	653
V. Accord.............................	11	375
VI. Discord............................	7	98
VII. Family Economics....................	16	355
VIII. Children............................	11	232
IX. Religion and Ethics..................	3	51
X. Miscellaneous.......................	7	200
All items................................	83	2,669

parents were living together. (See Table 10.) The result which appears in the last line in Table 7 (page 114) indicates that distribution of item and the presence or absence of separation and divorce probably were not associated.

FREQUENCY OF SUGGESTIONS IN CATEGORIES I, II, AND VII, AND OTHER FACTORS

Possible association between the number of suggestions in certain areas and relevant data usually available in school records was investigated. These included association of suggestions in Category VII—Family Economics with family income and marital status and in Category II—Two and Three Generation Adjustments with where the young person lived. The Chi-Square Test was applied to the hypothesis that there was no association between frequency of response in Category VII and estimated family income. The obtained chi-square was 12.69 as contrasted with the tabled chi-square of 26.22 for the same number of degrees of freedom at the $P_{.01}$ level of probability. In view of the small chi-square obtained it seemed reasonable to accept the hypothesis. To test the hypothesis that there was a significant difference

TABLE 11. *Association of Frequency of Free Response Items in Categories II, VI, and VII with Selected Factors*

CATEGORY AND FACTOR SELECTED FOR ANALYSIS	NUMBER OF PERSONS IN GROUP *	NUMBER OF ITEMS	MEAN SQUARE VARIATION		OBTAINED F	TABLED $F_{.01}$ FOR DEGREES OF FREEDOM CORRESPONDING TO OBTAINED F
			Between Groups	Within Groups		
Category II (unmarried participants only)						
Living with family	44	70	0.85	0.79	1.0	3.2
Not living with family.........	70	98				
Category VI						
Parents separated or divorced.....	6	7	0.05	0.21	4.2	6366.5
Parents together..	61	72				
Category VII						
Family income under $1,500....	44	64	0.52	0.55	1.1	6366.5
Family income over $5,000.....	38	49				
Married (alumni only)..........	21	25	0.07	0.55	7.9	6366.5
Unmarried (alumni only).........	43	54				

* Group includes all participants who reported the factor selected for analysis and who also suggested free response items in the particular category.

between the number of responses in Category VII and estimated family income under $1,500 and over $5,000, the analysis of variance technique was used. The findings appear in Table 11. Since the variance among individuals within the two groups was much larger than the variance between groups, there was no reason to believe that differences in frequency of items were associated with family income. It was also found that the difference was not significant between the number of persons whose family incomes were estimated to be under $3,000 and over $3,000 and who suggested items in Category VII. (See Table 12.)

The number of items dealing with family economics did not vary significantly between groups of married and single alumni. The

TABLE 12. *Percentage of Given Groups of Participants Who Suggested Items in Selected Areas Evaluated in Terms of the Difference in Percentage Between Groups*

Category	Group of Participants	Percentage of Total Number in the Group Who Suggested Items	Ratio of Difference in Percentage to Standard Deviation of Difference in Percentage
I. Family as a Social Institution............	Instruction in Sociology		
	Had course..........	23.8%	2.5
	No course...........	2.5	
II. Two and Three Generation Adjustments.	Unmarried:		
	Living with family...	17.9	0.3
	Not living with family	20.2	
VII. Family Economics..	Estimated family income:		
	Under $3,000........	45.8	0.9
	Over $3,000.........	40.1	
VII. Family Economics..	Estimated family income:		
	Under $1,500........	51.8	1.4
	Over $5,000........	36.2	
VII. Family Economics..	Married alumni........	60.0	1.63
	Unmarried alumni......	39.0	

variance among individuals was greater than the variance between groups. No significant difference appeared between married and unmarried alumni in the proportion of persons who suggested items relating to family economics.

There seemed to be no significant difference in the number of items suggested in Category II by unmarried participants who lived with their families and by those who did not. Data were handled so that freshman, senior, and alumni sub-groups were maintained in the analysis of variance. The obtained F was so much smaller than the tabled $F_{.01}$ for the corresponding numbers of degrees of freedom that the hypothesis was rejected that the difference was significant. Place of abode did not appear to be associated with the number of items dealing with adjustments between generations. With respect to those unmarried subjects who suggested items in this category there seemed to be no significant difference between the percentage of those responding among participants who lived with their families and those who did not live with their families.

Only one of the 39 persons suggesting items in Category I—The Family as a Social Institution gave more than one item. Although the difference in number of items per person suggested in this area was not significant, considerable difference was observed among those who had and had not taken sociology courses. Questions were suggested by 24 per cent of those who had been in sociology classes as contrasted with less than 3 per cent of those who had not studied in the field. The percentage difference is almost large enough to be considered statistically significant.

SUMMARY

Although the number and kind of items per person suggested by participants from the two colleges varied little, there were significant differences between the number suggested per person by men and by women, women tending to suggest the larger number. Seniors gave a larger number of suggestions per person than either freshmen or alumni.

The 2,752 items suggested by the total group were not evenly distributed among the 10 categories. Category IV—Sex received more items, and Category I—The Family as a Social Institution received fewer items than any other category. For freshmen, seniors, and alumni the distribution of items varied among categories. Freshmen suggested the largest number in Category III—Premarriage Problems, whereas seniors and alumni gave the largest number in the area of sex. The second largest number of items were given by freshmen to Category IV—Sex, by seniors to III—Premarriage Problems, and by alumni to V—Accord. Freshmen and alumni gave fewest suggestions in Category I—The Family as a Social Institution and seniors in Category IX—Religion and Ethics. Class and distribution of items among categories appeared to be associated.

More individuals suggested items in Category IV—Sex than in any other area. Although this category received 24 per cent of all items suggested, 63 per cent of all participants suggested at least one item in this category. The second largest number (47 per cent) of persons contributed items in Category III—Premarriage Problems. Few persons, less than 10 per cent, gave suggestions classified in Categories IX—Religion and Ethics and I—The Family as a Social Institution. Fewest persons gave suggestions in Category I, and the smallest proportion of items was received in this category.

The frequency of responses in the various categories varied enough between persons from "T" and "S" to indicate that the distribution was associated with the college in which the subjects were registered. For freshmen, college and distribution of items were associated. However, the distribution of items by "T" and "S" seniors and alumni varied so little that the differences were not statistically significant. "T" and "S" freshmen appeared to be much less homogeneous than seniors and alumni in the area distribution of the suggestions which they made.

Disregarding the college in which participants were registered, class and distribution of items appeared to be associated. A larger proportion of freshman than senior suggestions dealt with premarriage problems, religion and ethics, and adjustments between generations; only for the latter were differences sufficiently great to be considered statistically significant. However, there was sufficient evidence to assume that for freshman and senior groups, class and distribution of responses among categories were associated. The frequency of items in given areas suggested by seniors and by alumni varied more than between freshmen and seniors. Here, again, there is statistical evidence that class and distribution are associated. The chief sources of variation appeared to be in Categories III, V, VI, IX, and X. Seniors suggested a larger proportion of items than alumni in Category III—Premarriage Problems and also in IV—Discord. Alumni gave relatively greater response than seniors in Categories V—Accord, IX—Religion and Ethics, and X—Miscellaneous. Undergraduates and alumni differed significantly in the proportion of items dealing with adjustments between generations, undergraduates suggesting more items relating especially to "in-laws."

With reference to the number of items per person suggested in each area by freshmen, seniors, and alumni, there was little evidence of variation from class to class. Seniors gave a significantly larger number of items per person than freshmen in Category V—Accord. A significantly larger number of items per person were given to III—Premarriage Problems by undergraduates than by alumni.

There is no conclusive evidence of association of sex and distribution of items among categories with respect to senior and alumni men and women. However, there was evidence that men gave a significantly larger number of items than women in Category IV and that undergraduate women suggested a larger number of items dealing with adjustments between generations than did undergraduate men. Freshman women gave a significantly larger proportion of items than men in Categories II, V, and VI. However, it is questionable whether sex and distribution of items are associated with respect to the whole group of 632 subjects.

For freshman and senior subjects there was some evidence of association between the distribution of suggestions among categories and marital status in terms of single versus engaged. This was not true for alumni. Participants who were engaged to be married gave a larger proportion of items to Categories VII—Family Economics and V—Accord than persons who were single and not engaged. Those who were single and not engaged to be married gave a larger number of items to III—Premarriage Problems than those who were engaged and married. Married participants suggested a larger proportion of items in VII—Family Economics than the unmarried.

There is evidence that the ratings given to present family life and the distribution of free response items among categories are associated for the group as a whole and also for seniors and alumni. Freshmen who considered their family life less than satisfactory gave a larger proportion of their total response to Categories II—Two and Three Generation Adjustments and V—Accord than freshmen who gave more favorable ratings. However, persons whose parents were separated or divorced did not suggest a significantly larger proportion of items in VI—Discord than those whose parents were living together. It may be that problems of discord were no longer so acute because separation or divorce were partial solutions. The distribution of all items among categories revealed no evidence to support the hypothesis that frequency of suggestions in certain areas was associated with the fact that parents were together, separated, or divorced.

Family income and number of items suggested in Category VII—

Family Economics probably were not associated, whether the four income levels or only those over $5,000 and under $1,500 were considered. There was no evidence that married and single alumni gave a significantly different number of suggestions in this area. It is probable that there is no association between marital status and either the number of items in Category VII—Family Economics or the number of persons suggesting items in that area.

With regard to Category II—Two and Three Generation Adjustments, there appears to be no association between the number of items suggested in this category and the fact that unmarried participants lived with or away from their families. No evidence of association appears between place of abode and the number of persons suggesting items in Category II.

Only one subject gave more than one item in Category I—The Family as a Social Institution. However, the difference between the number of persons giving responses dealing with the family as a social institution who had and had not taken sociology courses approached statistical significance. Those who had received instruction in sociology courses more often suggested a topic in this area for discussion.

6:
Ratings of Specific Questions on Marriage and Family Life

In order to secure evaluations of specific aspects of marriage and family life as suitable topics for class discussion, a check list was presented to each participant. (See Appendix, page 181.) This list was composed of 28 questions, three from each category except Category IV—Sex, which was represented by four. Individual evaluation was not requested until each participant had written on the free response form his own ideas for instruction in marriage and family living. No limitation was placed on the time to be used for checking the list. All the 632 participants, with the exception of one, checked the list at least in part. If each of these persons evaluated each question, a total of 17,668 ratings might be expected. Ninety-nine per cent (17,479 ratings) of the possible total response was received. An average of 27.7 questions out of the total 28 were checked.

Since the first direction on the check list was "Read through the whole list and cross out any question that you do not understand," it is assumed that the persons who crossed out questions were following this direction. Questions 3 and 14, dealing with the history of the family and weaknesses of the family system, were the only ones to be crossed out by more than eight persons; seven were crossed out by none. Therefore, it is reasonable to assume that the questions were understood by the large majority of participants.

Little variation occurred between men and women and among freshmen, seniors, and alumni in the number of questions crossed out. In each class and sex they represented less than 1 per cent of the total number of questions presented for checking. These data are summarized in Table 13. The few questions neither checked nor crossed off

TABLE 13. *Number of Questions Rated, Crossed Out, and Omitted by 631 Participants Who Responded to the Check List*

COLLEGE, CLASS, AND SEX	NUMBER OF CHECK LIST QUESTIONS			
	Presented	Checked	Crossed Out	Omitted
"T" freshman men..........	2,156	2,133	13	10
"T" freshman women.......	532	529	2	1
"S" freshman men..........	4,760	4,680	34	46
"S" freshman women........	1,512	1,503	8	1
All freshmen..............	8,960	8,845	57	58
"T" senior men.............	1,428	1,424	3	1
"T" senior women..........	784	783		1
"S" senior men.............	1,456	1,440	1	15
"S" senior women..........	924	918	4	2
All seniors................	4,592	4,565	8	19
"T" alumni................	812	801	7	4
"T" alumnae...............	588	570	1	17
"S" alumni................	1,792	1,776	10	6
"S" alumnae...............	924	922	1	1
All alumni................	4,116	4,069	19	28
All "T" and "S" men.......	12,404	12,254	68	82
All "T" and "S" women....	5,264	5,225	16	23
All participants.............	17,668	17,479	84	105

were considered omitted. One freshman crossed off none and checked only the first nine questions. He therefore omitted questions 10 to 28 inclusive. Only 105 of the possible 17,668 ratings failed to solicit some type of response. Since cooperation was voluntary it is assumed that the check list held the interest of a large majority of the participants.

The range of the ratings on the five-point scale from 1 (Very Great Value) to 5 (No Value) indicates that the general trend was toward a favorable response. Of the 631 persons participating, 248 failed to give any question a rating as low as 5 (No Value). Twelve of these persons also avoided the other extreme and rated no question 1 (Very Great Value). However, these cautious persons represented only 2 per cent of the total group. More than half of the participants (350 or 55.3 per cent) used the full scale. Since most of the questions incorporated in the check list were chosen because of their frequency in the responses of experimental groups, it is not unreasonable to find a trend in mean ratings toward the favorable end of the scale.

Seniors and alumni differed little in the number of extremely favorable or unfavorable ratings given. A larger number of freshmen than seniors tended to rate extremely unfavorably. Only 18 per cent (59) of the freshmen as contrasted with 40 per cent (66) of the seniors failed to rate at least one question 5 (No Value). This percentage difference was significant ($P_1 - P_2/s_{P1} -_{P2} = 3$). Thirty per cent (51) of the alumni indicated that they believed no question warranted so low a rating as 5 (No Value). The variation between the percentage of seniors and the percentage of alumni who gave no ratings of 5 was too small to be considered significant. This was also true of the variation between freshmen, seniors, and alumni with regard to the proportion who considered no question of very great value as a topic for discussion. Only 10 freshmen, 10 seniors, and 11 alumni gave no ratings of 1 (Very Great Value).

The mean rating of each question for the total group of 631 participants appears in the last column of Table 14. The seven questions rated most favorably by the group as a whole are listed here in rank order, with the mean ratings placed in parentheses. The number preceding each question refers to its location on the check list.

Question 4. Exactly what should young people know about the anatomy and physiology of normal sex life? (1.64)

Question 10. What factors should be considered in choosing a mate? (1.71)

Question 15. How can natural sex drives of youth be directed when marriage must be delayed? (1.86)

Question 21. To what extent is success in marriage dependent upon the satisfactory adjustment of sex needs between husband and wife? (1.92)

Question 25. Exactly what should every young man and girl know about child care and child psychology? (1.97)

Question 27. What are the most common causes of marriage failure? (2.02)

Question 19. What adjustments may be made in courtship that will contribute to success in marriage? (2.13)

TABLE 14. *Mean Ratings of 28 Questions Concerning Marriage and Family*
1-Very Great Value

		COLLEGE		CLASS		
Number	Abbreviated Topic	"T"	"S"	Freshmen	Seniors	Alumni
3.	History of family	3.57	3.53	3.64	3.51	3.38
11.	Family in 1957	3.10	2.90	3.05	2.91	2.87
14.	Weaknesses of family system	3.12	2.90	2.99	3.07	2.89
8.	Adolescent maturity	2.58	2.61	2.65	2.52	2.59
24.	Freedom from family domination	2.52	2.68	2.74	2.61	2.40
26.	Opposing parents	2.70	2.81	2.73	2.61	2.83
1.	Youth popularity	2.68	2.53	2.48	2.60	2.80
10.	Choosing a mate	1.68	1.72	1.53	1.69	2.11
19.	Courtship adjustments	2.25	2.06	2.20	2.03	2.10
4.	Anatomy and physiology	1.68	1.62	1.59	1.46	**1.95**
15.	Sex adjustment where marriage delayed	1.79	1.90	1.97	1.71	1.80
21.	Role of sex in successful marriage	1.93	1.90	1.90	1.72	2.15
13.	Birth control arguments	2.25	2.31	2.37	1.99	2.44
9.	Sustaining personal interest in marriage	2.22	2.14	2.19	1.91	2.40
16.	Leisure interests of husband and wife	2.35	2.34	2.41	2.13	2.43
6.	Husband-wife domination	2.49	2.36	2.33	2.30	2.69
2.	Reconciling conflicting personalities	2.28	2.33	2.35	2.04	2.56
18.	Pros and cons of divorce	3.00	3.09	3.09	3.08	2.98
27.	Causes of marriage failures	1.99	2.04	1.96	1.86	2.34
5.	Women and career	2.65	2.54	2.49	2.47	2.90
20.	Risk in marrying on small income	2.66	2.47	2.54	2.48	2.60
22.	Just income division	2.29	1.67	2.29	2.14	2.13
12.	Role of small child in family	2.57	2.41	2.35	2.40	2.79
23.	Influence of early experiences on personality	2.16	2.15	2.19	2.10	2.16
25.	Needed knowledge of child care and psychology	2.07	1.92	1.95	1.83	2.17
7.	Family responsibility for religious life	2.94	2.71	2.72	2.65	3.13
17.	Contribution of religion to marriage success	2.91	2.69	2.59	2.87	3.04
28.	Hazard of religious differences	2.78	2.70	2.55	2.77	3.08

Life Presented to 631 Participants for Evaluation on a Five-Point Scale: to 5-No Value

Sex		Marital Status of Participant			Rating Assigned Family Life			Parents		All Participants
Men	Women	Single	Engaged	Married	Ideal	Successful-Satisfactory	Indifferent or Less	Separated or Divorced	Together	
3.41	3.66	3.52	3.84	3.45	3.50	2.57	3.69	3.56	3.54	3.54
2.99	2.93	2.94	3.25	3.08	2.95	2.99	2.78	2.84	2.98	2.97
3.04	2.86	2.98	3.04	3.05	2.85	3.06	2.79	2.74	3.00	2.99
2.61	2.58	2.58	2.77	2.62	2.62	2.60	2.51	3.00	2.59	2.60
2.68	2.49	2.62	2.83	2.44	2.67	2.73	2.15	2.89	2.62	2.62
2.74	2.84	2.63	3.19	3.37	2.78	2.75	2.68	3.42	2.70	2.72
2.61	2.53	2.52	3.13	2.82	2.37	2.55	3.03	2.53	2.59	2.59
1.66	1.82	1.63	2.00	2.38	1.67	1.66	1.82	1.74	1.71	1.71
2.40	2.05	2.16	1.85	2.13	2.11	2.16	2.01	2.33	2.13	2.13
1.61	1.71	1.62	1.66	1.97	1.63	1.60	1.66	1.74	1.64	1.64
1.83	1.93	1.86	1.79	1.95	2.15	1.80	1.77	1.95	1.86	1.86
1.91	1.92	1.87	1.98	2.39	1.88	1.90	1.84	2.05	1.91	1.92
2.32	2.21	2.27	2.38	2.34	2.25	2.31	2.24	2.26	2.29	2.29
2.23	2.03	2.16	2.11	2.33	2.16	2.16	2.24	1.68	2.18	2.17
2.37	2.27	2.35	2.09	2.59	2.28	2.35	2.37	2.32	2.34	2.34
2.42	2.38	2.39	2.47	2.42	2.33	2.47	2.27	2.11	2.41	2.40
2.35	2.24	2.29	2.43	2.56	2.26	2.38	1.99	2.26	2.32	2.32
3.06	3.06	3.02	3.40	3.21	2.77	3.15	2.99	2.26	3.09	3.06
2.02	2.04	2.00	1.96	2.49	1.94	2.06	1.89	2.05	2.02	2.02
2.71	2.27	2.57	2.49	2.79	2.42	2.57	2.84	2.42	2.59	2.58
2.59	2.41	2.53	2.46	2.67	2.35	2.52	2.88	2.79	2.53	2.54
2.26	2.11	2.23	2.08	2.18	2.18	2.24	2.09	2.47	2.21	2.22
2.48	2.44	2.42	2.79	2.67	2.22	2.46	2.75	2.44	2.47	2.47
2.17	2.13	2.15	2.31	2.05	2.16	2.18	2.08	2.05	2.16	2.16
1.96	2.00	1.95	2.12	2.05	1.94	1.99	2.67	2.21	1.96	1.97
2.79	2.80	2.75	3.00	3.13	2.41	2.60	2.84	2.42	2.81	2.79
2.79	2.71	2.73	3.06	2.92	2.47	2.78	2.88	3.79	2.77	2.77
2.73	2.72	2.63	3.25	3.46	2.70	2.68	2.76	3.05	2.72	2.73

Three of these seven questions (4, 15, and 21) were classified in Category IV—Sex, the category in which the largest number of free response items were suggested. Two of the seven questions (10 and 19) were classified in Category III—Premarriage Problems, in which the second largest number of free response items were suggested.

Question 4 was rated as one of very great value not only by the group as a whole but also by sub-groups made up of those from "S" and "T" colleges, in freshman, senior, and alumni classes, and of both sexes. The importance given to Question 4 suggests that the desire for more instruction in the anatomy and physiology of sex was urgent and widespread among the group. Question 10 (choosing a mate) also received extremely favorable ratings by young people from both colleges and sexes, and from the three classes. Freshmen gave Question 10 the most favorable mean rating of any question on the list. Questions 15 and 21 held third and fourth places among the seven questions with most favorable mean ratings. Although Question 15 (sex adjustment where marriage is delayed) held third place in rank order for the group as a whole, alumni gave it the most favorable mean rating of any question in the list. Since only 35 of the 148 alumni were married and their mean age was 24.87 years, it is reasonable that they should consider adjustments associated with delayed marriage extremely important.

Turning to the questions considered of least value, it is interesting to observe that the mean rating of none fell below 4 (Little Value). Only two of the 28 received mean ratings between 3 (Moderate Value) and 4 (Little Value) as rated by the group as a whole. Question 3 (history of the family) received a mean rating of 3.54, the least favorable mean rating on the list. Next in rank order was Question 18 (pros and cons of divorce) which received a mean rating of 3.06, close to Moderate Value. The questions whose mean ratings placed them among the seven considered of least value by the group as a whole were the three classified in Category I—The Family as a Social Institution, and those classified in Category IX—Religion. The seven questions with least favorable mean ratings are listed in rank order, with the mean ratings placed in parentheses after each.

Question 3. How does an understanding of the historical development of the family help the individual to adjust more successfully to new trends in family life today?   (3.54)

Question 18. From the point of view of society as a whole what are the arguments for and against divorce? (3.06)

Question 14. Is it possible to trace the most common difficulties of marriage to weaknesses in the family system? (2.99)

Question 11. In view of present social and economic trends what kind of family life will probably meet the needs of society in 1957? (2.97)

Question 7. What is the responsibility of the family for the religious life of its members? (2.79)

Question 17. To what extent does religion contribute to success in marriage? (2.77)

Question 28. Just how great a hazard is difference of religion in establishing lasting harmony in marriage? (2.73)

Question 3 received the least favorable rating not only by the group as a whole but also by the seven sub-groups. The relatively unfavorable mean ratings given Questions 14, 18, and 7 by the group as a whole were also verified by sub-groups from each college, class, and sex. All sub-groups except alumni agreed in placing Question 11 (the family in 1957) among the lowest seven in rank order.

Questions dealing with sex and premarriage problems were considered much more valuable for discussion than questions dealing with religion or the family as a social institution.

COLLEGE

The participants from "S" and "T" colleges rated the questions very much alike. Table 14 shows that the mean ratings by students and alumni from "S" and "T" varied little on 27 of the 28 questions. Greater variation on 13 questions appeared among individuals in the groups from each college than between the "S" and "T" groups themselves. These questions are indicated in Table 15 by enclosing the statistics in parentheses. Questions dealing with choice of mate, sex, and needed knowledge of child care and psychology were rated most valuable, and those dealing with the family as a social institution, divorce, and religion were rated least valuable by participants from both colleges. One question only received significantly different mean rat-

Question		RATIO OF LARGER TO SMALL MEAN SQUARE VARIANCE		
		College	Class	
Number	Abbreviated Topic	"T"—"S"	Freshmen Senior	Senior Alumni
3.	History of family	(5.6)	1.5	16.6 *
11.	Family in 1957	3.2	1.3	(15.4)
14.	Weaknesses of family system	5.3	(1.8)	20.0 *
8.	Adolescent maturity	(10.6)	1.3	(3.7)
24.	Freedom from family domination	2.5	1.2	25.0 *
26.	Opposing parents	1.0	(1.3)	1.6
1.	Youth popularity	2.6	1.2	2.4
10.	Choosing a mate	(5.1)	2.8	10.0 *
19.	Courtship adjustments	4.4	2.6	(3.0)
4.	Anatomy and physiology	(1.7)	2.6	20.0 *
15.	Sex adjustment where marriage delayed	1.6	6.7	(1.6)
21.	Role of sex in successful marriage	(8.4)	3.7	11.1 *
13.	Birth control arguments	(3.1)	10.0 *	10.0 *
9.	Sustaining personal interest in marriage	(1.4)	7.7 *	14.3 *
16.	Leisure interests of husband and wife	(126.3)	7.1 *	5.6
6.	Husband-wife domination	1.6	(14.3)	7.1 *
2.	Reconciling conflicting personalities	(4.0)	7.7 *	16.7 *
18.	Pros and cons of divorce	(1.4)	(160.6)	(2.0)
27.	Causes of marriage failures	(3.4)	(1.0)	14.0 *
5.	Women and career	1.2	(35.6)	10.0 *
20.	Risk in marrying on small income	3.4	(4.0)	(1.3)
22.	Just income division	20.0 *	1.9	(118.7)
12.	Role of small child in family	3.2	(3.9)	10.0 *
23.	Influence of early experiences on personality	(109.0)	(1.2)	(4.0)
25.	Needed knowledge of child care and psychology	3.1	1.6	8.0 *
7.	Family responsibility for religious life	4.8	(2.8)	10.0 *
17.	Contribution of religion to marriage success	4.6	5.9	1.4
28.	Hazard of religious differences	(1.9)	3.0	4.2

Note. Values for the ratio placed in parentheses (the obtained *F*) indicate that the the appropriate tabled value of $F_{.01}$ was 6366.48, as read from Table XXXV, Snedecor, Inc., Ames, Iowa, 1934. Where the value for the ratio is not in parentheses the variance $F_{.01}$ was 6.7. Figures with asterisks indicate values larger than tabled values of $F_{.01}$.

OF RATINGS ASSIGNED BY GIVEN GROUPS OF PARTICIPANTS

Sex	Marital Status		Rating of Family Life		PARENTS LIV-ING TOGETHER
Men Women	Single Engaged	Unmarried Married	Ideal Successful and Satisfactory	Satisfactory or Better Indifferent or Worse	LIVING BUT NOT TOGETHER
5.6	3.7	(3.6)	12.5 *	12.5 *	(128.3)
(3.7)	2.6	(3.4)	(12.5)	1.6	(4.6)
3.2	(7.5)	(9.9)	2.9	3.6	(1.0)
(11.5)	1.3	(138.3)	(45.4)	(2.6)	2.2
3.2	1.4	(1.0)	(4.8)	14.3 *	(1.1)
(1.3)	7.7 *	8.3 *	(21.6)	(5.5)	4.8
(1.5)	14.3 *	1.8	2.3	12.5 *	(18.1)
2.9	6.3	16.7 *	(107.7)	1.5	(588.5)
25.0*	3.8		(5.6)	1.2	(1.7)
1.5	(10.4)	5.3	(9.8)	(3.4)	(4.8)
1.4	(4.6)	(3.7)	10.00 *	(16.4)	(7.4)
(109.5)	(1.8)	8.3 *	(35.0)	(4.6)	(3.0)
(1.0)	(2.8)	(12.6)	(5.2)	(5.2)	(81.6)
4.2	(10.4)	(1.2)		(3.1)	3.6
1.0	2.6	2.0	(2.5)	(41.8)	(126.3)
(7.3)	(4.9)	(154.6)	1.1	1.6	1.1
1.1	(1.5)	1.7	(1.2)	7.1 *	(20.5)
	4.4	(1.7)	7.7 *	1.0	8.3 *
(24.8)	(15.3)	7.7 *	1.0	1.5	(61.9)
16.7 *	(4.8)	1.2	1.3	3.2	(2.8)
2.8	(6.6)	(2.1)	1.6	5.3	(1.2)
2.4	(1.2)	(20.7)	(4.0)	1.2	1.0
(5.5)	5.9	1.5	4.4	4.8	(57.8)
(5.2)	1.1	(2.5)	(35.7)	(1.7)	(5.0)
(5.0)	1.3	(4.5)	(4.9)	50.0*	1.1
(165.8)	2.7	2.9	1.2	1.4	1.7
(1.9)	3.4	(1.7)	5.6	(2.4)	12.5 *
(177.0)	11.1 *	12.5 *	(55.9)	(4.2)	1.1

variance among participants within groups was the greater mean square and, therefore, G. W. *Calculation and Interpretation of Analyses of Variance and Covariance.* Collegiate Press, between groups was the greater mean square and the tabled value of $F_{.05}$ was 3.9 and of

ings from the two groups. This was Question 22 (just income division), given a mean rating of 1.67 by participants from "S" and 2.29 by participants from "T." Association between ratings and college is accepted for this question only because the variation is greater than can be ascribed to chance alone. It is interesting to note that Question 22 was rated significantly more valuable by persons from "S" than "T," although "S" students and alumni came from homes where the total family income was larger. It may be that "S" subjects were more concerned about the strains and tensions that frequently accompany the adjustment of living standards required by small initial salaries.

CLASS IN COLLEGE

In many cases freshmen, seniors, and alumni gave similar evaluation. Ratings varied so little for nine of the 28 questions that differences were probably due to chance variation. All classes agreed in rating Questions 19 (courtship adjustments), 22 (just income division), and 23 (influences of childhood experiences on personality) close to Great Value. Questions 11 (the family in 1957) and 18 (the pros and cons of divorce) were not considered valuable by any group. General agreement also occurred on Questions 1 (youth popularity), 8 (adolescent maturity), 20 (the risk of marrying on a small income), and 26 (opposing parents). These mean ratings are given in Table 14 on page 132.

Such similar ratings were given by freshmen and seniors to 22 of the 28 questions that the results of analyses of variance indicate no reason to believe that rating and class are associated. There is evidence that undergraduate class and question rating are associated in the cases of Questions 2, 9, 13, and 16. There is also rather doubtful evidence of association relative to Questions 15 and 17. On all four questions where rating and class appear to be associated, seniors gave more favorable mean ratings than freshmen. These were Questions 9 (sustaining personal interest in marriage), 13 (birth control arguments), 16 (leisure interests of husband and wife) and 2 (reconciling conflicting personalities). It seems reasonable that seniors should rate these more favorably than freshmen since the questions deal with problems that concern young people of the age when many of their contemporaries marry. The fact that seniors tended to rate questions dealing with sex and accord more favorably than freshmen is consistent with the findings, reported on page 118, that seniors also gave a proportionately larger number of suggestions in these areas.

Seniors and alumni varied more frequently in mean rating of individual questions than freshmen and seniors. Significant differences between mean ratings by seniors and alumni were found for 15 questions as contrasted with significant differences on four questions in the comparison of freshman and senior ratings. Corresponding variations were also observed in the number and distribution of written suggestions. The specific questions where senior ratings differed markedly from the ratings by alumni were scattered among all nine categories. On two additional questions, 16 (the leisure interests of husband and wife) and 28 (the hazard to success in marriage created by religious differences), the mean ratings varied sufficiently to indicate that association between rating and class is open to question. In both cases seniors gave more favorable ratings than alumni. To only three of the 15 questions did alumni give significantly more favorable ratings than seniors. They were Questions 3 (history of the family), 14 (weaknesses of the family system), and 24 (freedom from family domination). The more favorable alumni rating given to Questions 3 and 14 may reflect the fact that a larger proportion of alumni than seniors had taken one or more courses in sociology. It is interesting that alumni, who are generally expected by society to establish their independence, rated "How does one free himself, without quarreling, from excessive family domination?" higher on the scale than did seniors.

Seniors gave significantly more favorable ratings than alumni to 12 of the 28 questions and considered the discussion of three of these much more valuable than did either freshmen or alumni. These were questions in which young people contemplating marriage might have a special interest, namely, Questions 2 (reconciling conflicting personalities), 9 (sustaining personal interest in marriage), and 13 (birth control arguments). The nine other questions on which senior and alumni mean ratings varied more than can be ascribed to chance alone were Questions 10 (choosing a mate), 4 (anatomy and physiology), 21 (role of sex in marriage success), 6 (husband-wife domination), 27 (causes of marriage failure), 5 (women and career), 12 (role of small child in family), 25 (needed knowledge of child care and psychology), and 7

(family responsibility for religious life). In each case senior ratings
were more favorable than those given by alumni. Whereas undergraduate groups agreed more often than they disagreed, seniors and
alumni differed significantly in their estimated values of more than
half of the questions.

SEX DIFFERENCES

Men and women varied little in ratings given to questions concerning sex. The differences in the mean ratings for 24 of the 28 questions could be expected from chance variation. However, for two questions, 3 (history of the family) and 9 (sustaining personal interest in
marriage), the evidence is not conclusive. Although men appeared to
rate Question 3 and women Question 9 more favorably, the variance
may have been a matter of chance rather than association.

Sufficient evidence appeared to support the hypothesis of association
of rating with sex in only two questions, 5 (women and career) and
19 (courtship adjustments). Women tended to rate both as of greater
value than did men. The ratings assigned by men and women gave
little evidence of association between rating and sex when subjected to
analysis of variance. This is consistent with the findings reported on
page 118 relative to the distribution of suggestions given by men and
women.

MARITAL STATUS

Single, engaged, and married participants were more often similar
than different in their value ratings of questions on the check list. All
tended to give very favorable ratings to Questions 4 (anatomy and
physiology) and 15 (sex adjustment where marriage is delayed), while
Questions 26 (opposing parents) and 28 (hazard of religious differences) received relatively unfavorable ratings from all three groups.
For only six of the 28 questions were differences in mean rating large
enough to indicate an association between rating and marital status of
the participant.

Engaged persons and those not engaged differed significantly in
their ratings on only three questions, namely, 1, 26, and 28. Question 1

reads: "How can a young person make himself more popular with other young people?" The mean rating given this question by the latter group was so much more favorable than the rating given by the engaged persons that there is reason to believe rating and engagement are associated. This question was chosen to represent Category III— Premarriage Problems, wherein participants not engaged gave a significantly larger proportion of free response items than those who were engaged. The findings are consistent in this case.

These two groups also differed significantly in mean ratings given to Questions 26 (opposing parents) and 28 (hazard of religious differences). In each case the mean ratings by persons not engaged were more favorable. It is possible that the young people who were engaged to be married had, at least in the choice of a mate, come to a decision with regard to the hazard of religious differences and the wisdom of opposing parents. A noticeable variation in mean ratings by the two groups appears in Table 14 (page 132) for Questions 12 (role of the small child in the family) and 10 (choosing a mate). In each case the group not engaged to be married gave the more favorable mean rating. However, these differences were not sufficiently large to establish statistically the hypothesis that rating and engagement are associated.

The evaluations by married and unmarried participants were analyzed. Ratings and marital status appear to be associated with respect to only five questions, namely, 10 (choosing a mate), 26 (opposing parents), 27 (causes of marriage failure), 28 (hazard of religious differences), and 21 (role of sex in successful marriage). In each case, unmarried persons gave the more favorable mean ratings. This is logical, since it is probable that those who were married had discovered or worked out at least partial answers for these questions in their own experience.

RATING OF FAMILY LIFE

It seemed reasonable to assume that the person's degree of satisfaction with his family life and his evaluation of questions proposed for discussion might be associated. This assumption was tested by analysis of variance. To facilitate statistical manipulation the seven categories used in evaluating family life were grouped in three units: (*a*) ideal, (*b*) successful and satisfactory, and (*c*) less than satisfactory. To (*c*) were assigned the categories indifferent, unsatisfactory, unsuccessful, and breaking. Mean ratings given questions by the 108 persons who considered their present family life ideal were compared with the ratings given by 421 persons who indicated family life as successful or satisfactory. Evidence of association was found for only three of the 28 questions, 3 (history of the family), 15 (sex adjustment where marriage is delayed), and 18 (pros and cons of divorce). The question on divorce was considered more valuable by those rating family life ideal than by those who were either less satisfied or more restrained in their evaluation of present family life. Those who considered their family life ideal gave less favorable ratings to the other two questions. Question 3 received the least favorable mean rating of all questions from those who considered their present family life ideal.

The mean ratings given by the 76 subjects who stated that their family life was less than satisfactory varied little from the mean ratings given by those claiming successful or satisfactory family life. For only five of the 28 questions is it reasonable to assume that the two evaluations are associated. The ratings given may reflect possible reasons for the dissatisfaction. The mean ratings of Questions 24 (freedom from family domination) and 2 (reconciling conflicting personalities), given by those who reported family life unfavorably, indicated that they considered a discussion of these questions much more valuable than did those who considered their family life satisfactory or better. These two questions may have represented basic issues in discord that participants witnessed or experienced.

Association between ratings of questions and family life was evident for Questions 1 (how to be more popular), 3 (the history of the family), and 25 (child care and psychology). These questions were rated significantly more favorably by those satisfied with family life than by those who were dissatisfied. In two questions, 12 (role of small child in the family) and 20 (risk of marrying on a small income), the differences in mean ratings were not quite large enough to make it reasonable to assume that ratings of questions and family life were associated. In both cases those dissatisfied with family life gave the more unfavorable rating to the question.

The variations between the groups in mean ratings of items classified according to the participant's evaluation of his present family life were more frequently due to chance than to association between the two factors analyzed.

SEPARATION OR DIVORCE OF PARENTS

The probability of association between the mean ratings of certain questions and separation or divorce of parents was investigated. Only 19 of the 632 participants reported that their parents were separated or divorced. The two questions in which mean rating and separation or divorce appear to be associated are Questions 18 (pros and cons of divorce) and 17 (contribution of religion to marriage success). Participants from homes broken by separation or divorce seemed to consider a discussion of divorce of greater value to them personally than young people from unbroken homes.

Although this is reasonable, it is not consistent with the finding reported in Table 10 on page 122, which shows very little difference in the number of free response items dealing with discord received from those whose parents were separated or divorced and from those whose parents were together. Those whose parents lived together rated Question 17 (the contribution of religion to marriage success) of more value than those whose parents were separated or divorced. Doubtful evidence of association between question rating and separation or divorce of parents was shown for one additional question, 26 (opposing parents). As might be expected, those whose parents were living together considered this question more valuable for discussion than those whose parents were separated or divorced.

For 18 of the 28 questions the variation among members of the two groups was greater than the variation between groups. Except for two questions, there is no reason to assume that question rating and separation or divorce of parents are associated.

SOCIOLOGY INSTRUCTION

Evidence of association between question rating and presence or absence of sociology instruction was sought for Questions 3, 11, 14, and 18. Those who had taken sociology courses tended to give somewhat

TABLE 16. *Association of Ratings Assigned Eleven Questions with Selected Traits of Participants as Indicated by Analysis of Variance**

QUESTION		Trait and Classification of Participant	Number of Persons in Group	Mean Rating of Question	MEAN SQUARE VARIATION		Obtained F	Tabled Value of $F_{.01}$ for Degrees of Freedom Corresponding to Obtained F
Number	Abbreviated Topic				Between Groups	Among Persons within Groups		
	Instruction in Sociology							
3.	History of family	Had course	265	3.40	3.90	1.27	3.07	3.05
		No course	348	3.65				
11.	Family in 1957	Had course	268	2.94	0.84	1.75	2.08	9.02
		No course	356	3.00				
14.	Weaknesses of family system	Had course	263	3.01	0.17	1.28	7.53	9.02
		No course	345	2.98				
18.	Pros and cons of divorce	Had course	269	3.13	7.48	1.59	4.70	3.05
		No course	357	3.01				
	Place of abode							
24.	Freedom from family domination	With family	244	2.54	0.004	1.40	350.00	9.02
		Not with family	346	2.59				
8.	Adolescent maturity	With family	243	2.54	1.77	1.44	1.23	3.05
		Not with family	342	2.70				
26.	Opposing parents	With family	245	2.67	0.02	2.02	101.00	9.02
		Not with family	345	2.69				

Employment of mother other than homemaking							
5. Women and career	Employed	61	2.51	0.02	1.45	72.50	9.02
	Not employed	561	2.58				
22. Just income division	Employed	61	2.16	0.27	1.23	4.56	9.02
	Not employed	566	2.22				
Estimated family income							
5. Women and career	Under $1,500	85	2.68	0.66	1.58	2.39	9.02
	Over $5,000	104	2.48				
22. Just income division	Under $1,500	84	2.18	1.17	1.34	1.15	9.02
	Over $5,000	104	2.35				
15. Sex adjustment where marriage delayed	Under $1,500	83	1.71	0.86	0.96	1.12	9.02
	Over $5,000	103	1.87				
20. Risk in marrying on small income	Under $1,500	85	2.78	9.16	1.55	5.91	3.11
	Over $5,000	103	2.31				

* Tabled values of $F_{.01}$ were read from Table XXXV, Snedecor, G. W. *Calculation and Interpretation of Analyses of Variance and Covariance.* Collegiate Press, Inc., Ames, Iowa, 1934. Tabled values of $F_{.01}$ less than 4.00 indicate that the greater mean square was found to be the variance between groups. College classes, namely, freshman, senior, alumni, were used as sub-groups in the analyses.

more favorable ratings than those who had not to Questions 3 (history of the family) and 11 (the family in 1957). However, only in Question 3 were differences significant and even here the statistic was very close to the critical point. These data appear in Table 16. Less favorable ratings were given to Questions 14 (weaknesses of the family system) and 18 (pros and cons of divorce) by students of sociology than by those who had taken no courses in this field. The difference in mean ratings for Question 18 (pros and cons of divorce) was sufficiently large to indicate that question rating and instruction in sociology are associated. However, it should be observed (Table 16) that the mean ratings for all four questions by both groups were considerably below the median. The fact that the variations in mean ratings for Questions 11 and 14 were too small to justify acceptance of the hypothesis of association between question rating and sociology instruction is consistent with the difference of doubtful significance observed between the number of persons who gave suggestions in Category I—The Family as a Social Institution and groups of participants who had and had not taken courses in sociology.

PLACE OF ABODE

Three questions dealing with adjustments between persons of different generations were analyzed to ascertain whether there was evidence of association between the mean rating of the question and the fact that the participant was or was not living with his family at the time of response. The three questions were Questions 24 (freedom from family domination), 8 (adolescent maturity), and 26 (opposing parents). While in each case the persons who were living with their families considered the questions more valuable for discussion than those who were not, in no case was the evidence sufficient to assume that the differences arose from factors other than individual differences. Table 16 shows that the variation among members within groups was much greater than the variation in ratings between groups for Questions 24 and 26. Although the variation between groups in the case of Question 8 was greater than among individuals within groups, the variance was not sufficiently large to warrant accepting the hypothesis that rating and the place where the participant was living were associated.

This is consistent with the findings reported in Chapter V. Place of abode did not appear to be associated either with the number of items suggested or with the percentage of subjects giving responses in Category II—Two and Three Generation Adjustments.

FAMILY INCOME

The probability of association between family income and mean ratings of questions dealing with family economics and delayed marriage was investigated. Although the differences were not significant because of the wide variation among individuals, persons whose family incomes were estimated below $1,500 per year tended to give somewhat more favorable mean ratings to Questions 22 (just income division) and 15 (sex adjustment where marriage is delayed) than those with incomes over $5,000 per year. The reverse was true of mean ratings given Questions 5 (women and career) and 20 (risk of marrying on a small income). Participants who estimated family income to be over $5,000 per year considered Question 20 more valuable for discussion than those whose family income was below $1,500 per year. In this case alone the variance between groups was significantly greater than within groups. Question 20 reads: "When young people have been accustomed to much at home, are they wise to risk marriage on a small income?" It is easy to understand why persons from families whose annual income is over $5,000 should consider discussion of this question more valuable than those from families whose annual income is less than $1,500.

MOTHER'S OCCUPATION

Two questions dealing with family economics, Questions 5 (women and career) and 22 (just income division), were analyzed to see if mean ratings were associated with employment of the mother outside the home. For both questions the mean ratings given by participants whose mothers were employed outside the home were slightly more favorable than the mean ratings given by those whose mothers were homemakers only. These data appear in Table 16 on page 144. For neither question can it be assumed the mother's occupation and the mean ratings given questions are associated.

SUMMARY

The responses on the check list were unusually complete. Very few questions were crossed off or omitted. Over half of the participants used the full scale from 1 (Very Great Value) to 5 (No Value). Many more ratings were favorable than unfavorable. Whereas nine out of 10 persons rated at least one question 1 (Very Great Value), only four out of 10 persons gave any question a rating as low as 5 (No Value).

Questions considered most valuable for discussion by the group as a whole were Questions 4 (anatomy and physiology), 10 (choosing a mate), 15 (sex adjustment where marriage is delayed), 21 (role of sex in successful marriage), and 25 (needed knowledge of child care and psychology). Those considered least valuable by the group as a whole were Questions 3 (history of the family) and 18 (pros and cons of divorce). The questions receiving the most favorable mean rating by each class were Questions 10 (choosing a mate) by freshmen, 4 (anatomy and physiology) by seniors, and 15 (sex adjustment where marriage is delayed) by alumni. Question 3 (history of the family) received the least favorable mean rating given by each class.

Participants from "S" and "T" varied significantly in mean rating on only one question, 22 (just income division). Persons from "S" tended to consider the question more valuable for discussion than those from "T." Freshmen and seniors varied little in their ratings. The four questions on which seniors and freshmen differed significantly were Questions 2 (reconciling conflicting personalities), 9 (sustaining personal interest in marriage), 13 (birth control arguments), and 16 (leisure interests of husband and wife). In each case seniors gave more favorable ratings. Seniors and alumni differed in their value ratings more often than they agreed. Alumni gave more favorable ratings than seniors to Questions 3 (history of the family), 14 (weaknesses of the family system), and 24 (freedom from family domination). Twelve questions were considered more valuable for discussion by seniors than by alumni. Seniors gave more favorable ratings to Questions 9 (sustaining personal interest in marriage) and 13 (birth control arguments) than did either freshmen or alumni. The evaluation of questions varied more between classes than between colleges.

Sex and value ratings were associated for only two questions, 5 (women and career) and 19 (courtship adjustments). In both cases women gave more favorable ratings than men. The marital status of the participant appeared to have little relationship to question ratings. Those persons not engaged to be married considered discussion of Questions 1 (youth and popularity), 26 (opposing parents), and 28 (hazard of religious differences) more valuable than those who were engaged or married. Unmarried participants gave more favorable ratings than those who were married to Questions 10 (choosing a mate), 7 (family responsibility for religious life), and 21 (role of sex in successful marriage). Sex and marital status were less often associated with the rating assigned questions than was class in college.

The degree of satisfaction with family life at home and the value ratings assigned questions were not associated for the majority of persons. Those who considered their family life indifferent or unsatisfactory tended to rate Questions 2 (reconciling conflicting personalities) and 24 (freedom from family domination) more valuable than did the remainder of the group. This was not true with reference to Questions 18 (pros and cons of divorce).

Whether the parents of participants were separated, divorced, or living together did not seem to be associated with the rating of questions. The 19 persons whose parents were separated or divorced considered Question 18 (pros and cons of divorce) more valuable and Question 17 (contribution of religion to marriage success) less valuable than persons whose parents were living together. Question 18 was also considered more valuable by those who had not taken college courses in sociology than by those who had studied in this field.

There seemed to be no association between the value ratings assigned Questions 8 (recognition of adolescent maturity), 24 (freedom from family domination), and 26 (opposing parents), and the fact that participants lived with their families or away from home. The relative value placed on Question 5 (women and career) varied little between those whose mothers were or were not employed outside the home. The level of family income and ratings of Questions 5 (women and career), 22 (just income division), and 15 (sex adjustment where marriage is delayed), were not associated. However, those persons with family incomes over $5,000 tended to rate Question 20 (risk in marrying on a small income) more valuable than those with family incomes under $1,500.

Although the check list revealed less variation between groups than did the free response form, the direction of variation tended to be the same throughout.

7:
Conclusions and Implications

W HEN given an opportunity to suggest what they believe are important problems and questions for consideration in education for marriage and family living young men and women respond eagerly and constructively. They know quite clearly what they want to learn and they are able to give specific suggestions for making the instruction most helpful. The suggestions and evaluations of young women and young men reflect thoughtful discrimination and a genuine effort to express themselves honestly and objectively.

The recommendations given by young people in this study tend to center around human relations rather than material resources. For instance, young adults are more concerned about the kind of person to marry than about the amount of money needed to establish a home and provide security. They are more concerned with specific situations than with generalizations, and with personal problems rather than with social theory. Few questions deal with the field of genetics, but many were asked concerning the inheritance of certain characteristics obviously possessed by an acquaintance. The problems of older youth appear to be closely related to their own personal experiences and anxieties.

The approach of young people to questions concerning marriage and family life is more often positive than negative. There is much more interest in learning how to make marriage successful than in learning ways of resolving discord. Young men and women want to know what should be discussed before marriage, how to establish satisfying patterns of adjustment between husband and wife, and how to plan for children. There is much greater concern with how to get along with parents than with making them over or "bringing-up-father." Questions involving the development of harmonious relationships with relatives are asked much more often than "must we marry orphans?" Both the written suggestions and the value ratings of questions submitted on the check list suggest general acceptance of the idea that education for marriage is possible and desirable.

WHAT YOUNG ADULTS WANT TO LEARN ABOUT MARRIAGE AND FAMILY LIVING*

Young people have many unanswered questions about sex.** More individuals proposed questions or suggestions dealing with sex than with any other topic, and more separate items were received in this than in any other category. The check list findings also indicate a widespread desire for more discussion of sex facts and adjustments. Although other investigators studying older youth report "choice of mate" and "starting boy-girl relationships" as areas of foremost concern (see page 20), the findings of this study tend to support Folsom's conclusion that sex is a primary concern. Folsom writes: "Students show clearly, both through questionnaires and through their attendance where lectures are voluntary, that sex information is what they chiefly want. This is not an indication of morbidity but simply of the fact that reliable sex information has been difficult to get." [15 : 139]

Young people today ask for realistic and functional family life education centered around their problems of living in this modern world. The traditional stress laid on the history of the family, divorce, and family disorganization is not the emphasis desired by most of those participating in this study. This may reflect ignorance of the potential contribution of the traditional approach as well as a conviction that it has little to offer. Nevertheless, the conclusion that these young people are more concerned with many other aspects of education for marriage is inescapable.

The interests and needs of freshmen and seniors as revealed by their suggestions for family life education are similar in many areas. It is likely that seniors are more acutely concerned with preparation for marriage since they gave more suggestions, and a larger proportion of these dealt with accord in marital adjustments. Freshmen appear to be

---

* Summaries of findings appear in Chapters V and VI on pages 125 and 148.

** See definition in the "Outline for the Classification of Free Response Items in Categories," Appendix, page 175.

more concerned with premarriage problems. However, the frequency of freshman and senior suggestions in large areas varied little. The similarity was also striking in undergraduate responses to the check list, for ratings varied significantly on fewer than one in five questions.

The marked individual differences within groups suggest that instruction in large classes probably could not adequately care for individual needs. Freshmen varied more within their own group than did seniors or alumni. Whether the greater differences observed among freshmen are real or merely more apparent is not known, although there are greater differences in background traits among freshmen than among seniors. It is probable that many selective factors operate between the freshman and the senior year to render the senior group more homogeneous in response. The findings of this study led to the conclusion that freshmen have a wide variety of perplexities with regard to marriage and family living, and that they as well as seniors are eager for effective instruction in this field.

The fact that the participants from the two colleges varied significantly in a number of background traits (see Appendix, Part I) suggests the possibility of considerable variation in what young persons from the two institutions consider important. Differences between college groups were more apparent in the written suggestions than on the check list. There is, however, sufficient evidence of variation between the colleges to warrant considering each as a separate unit in analyzing needs and making plans for instruction in marriage and family living.

Young men and women seem to agree in what they want to learn in this field. Although the young women tended to give more suggestions per person, the kinds of suggestions differed little from those proposed by men. On the check list marked variations in value ratings were evident only for those questions dealing with marriage versus career and courtship adjustments. The similarity of the responses of men and women makes it seem reasonable to offer instruction to mixed groups.

ADEQUACY OF TECHNIQUES AND INSTRUMENTS

Since they tend to secure frank, sincere, and discriminating responses from young men and women in and out of college, the techniques developed in this study for the exploration of questions of young adults in the field of marriage and family life appear to be effective. They are feasible for use in ascertaining the suggestions and questions considered important by members of study groups and classes and by isolated individuals who cannot be approached directly. Areas of greatest and least concern revealed in written responses and those indicated on the check list were essentially the same.

The reason for the apparent lack of association between suggestions or value ratings in selected areas and related background traits may be that the instruments and methods of analysis are not sufficiently sensitive to detect small but real differences. There is some evidence to support this point of view. Youth from broken homes, for instance, although their written suggestions did not appear to place greater emphasis on family accord or discord, gave higher value ratings to the question on divorce than did those from unbroken homes. Although groups of young people classified on the basis of four levels of family income gave much the same emphasis to family economics, those from families with incomes over $5,000 and under $1,500 placed quite different values on discussion of "the risk of marrying on a small income."

Fewer significant differences between sub-groups were observed through the check list, although the findings are generally consistent with those revealed on the free response form. Before the check list is used independently of the free response form it should be expanded to include a larger number and a greater variety of questions. It may then be useful as a device for determining changes in the evaluation of certain problems before and after instruction in this field.

IMPLICATIONS FOR PLANNING FUNCTIONAL INSTRUCTION IN MARRIAGE AND FAMILY LIVING

Instruction of youth for marriage and family living should utilize as one source of help in developing a program, the recommendations of young people themselves. Young adults in and out of college can raise many specific questions and give constructive suggestions significant to the group as a whole in planning and evaluating instruction. These resources of thinking and experience should be used in curriculum planning.

Instruction in marriage and family living should take into account the areas of greatest and least importance as judged by the particular group concerned. Although questions dealing with sex, premarriage adjustments, accord, and family economics appear to interest a relatively large number of young adults, the participants from the two colleges varied significantly in areas of concern. It is probable that differences between other college groups would be observed if the study were extended to include a larger number of institutions. No single outline or course of study will meet the needs of different groups with equal effectiveness. Major consideration should be given to those questions which perplex members of the group most acutely and most frequently.

Admission to study groups and classes in marriage and family life should be based on the person's need and readiness rather than on his class or chronological age. The questions and suggestions for instruction considered important by freshmen and by seniors are very similar; freshmen frequently demonstrated as much maturity, insight, and acuteness of concern as did seniors. There seems, therefore, to be little justification for the current practice of limiting enrollment in courses in marriage and the family to upperclassmen.

Discussion leaders and teachers in the field of education for marriage and family living should be familiar with the resources of and the recent findings in many related fields. A wide range of knowledge is covered by instruction which deals with questions that perplex young adults, questions which touch many fields and relate to material from diverse sources. Leaders should have a broad background and be qualified to locate and evaluate pertinent data in the humanities, arts, and sciences; and they must be able to present objectively and to interrelate widely different points of view on controversial issues. The question of whether instruction in marriage and family life shall be the responsibility of one person alone, of a coordinator who uses specialists on appropriate occasions, or of a group of specialists, is one on which there is great difference of opinion; but, regardless of that question, the resources of many fields must be made available if one is to provide a truly functional program of family education and preparation for marriage.

IMPLICATIONS IN FIELDS CONTRIBUTING TO EDUCATION
FOR MARRIAGE AND FAMILY LIVING

Effective education for marriage and family living is an all-college function involving many disciplines. The perplexities and concerns of college youth bring into focus contributions from many fields of learning. The questions asked and rated as important in the area of marriage and family life tend to deal with whole experiences rather than with one aspect as defined by traditional course or subject matter lines. In asking how to get along with others, young men and women want to know about the physiological, psychological, and emotional foundations of behavior; the significance of likenesses and differences in the thinking and feeling of men and women; what society demands of individuals and why; and the hazards to successful adjustment in family life inherent in different interests, values, social experiences, personality traits, intellectual resources, and standards of living. Such a problem draws upon knowledge from the fields of biological and physical sciences, psychology, psychiatry, sociology, philosophy, and economics. It uses basic information, generalizations, appreciations, and understandings developed in other disciplines and integrates all available resources in terms of the particular problem in mind. No one discipline can answer adequately the wide range of questions in the field of marriage and family life. The recommendations of young adults concerning instruction in marriage and the family have direct implications for instruction in fields such as biology, hygiene, psychology, home economics, sociology, and economics.

The questions of college youth suggest that hygiene classes should make available more specific information on the anatomy and physiology of sex. In biology classes exclusive emphasis on the structure and function of organisms other than the human being is questioned. A need for greater understanding of conception, of the birth and growth of children, and of physical changes in adolescence, maturity, and senility is quite evident. Young adults seek an objective analysis of the role of sex in the life of the individual, the family, and the community.

The importance of more emphasis in psychology on the wholeness of human experience rather than on isolated reactions, animal behavior, and mechanistic theory was apparent. Young people want more direct help in understanding self, the development of personality, and the role of emotions in adjustment. They reveal many anxieties concerning changing parent-child, sibling, and mate relationships in the family group. Youth wants to understand and learn how to use wisely the principles of mental hygiene, controls of group behavior, and psychological factors in promoting effective social action.

The recognition that the skills, techniques, and materials of the home are important only to the degree that they implement or thwart satisfying adjustment within the family has significant implications for instruction in home economics. That homemaking is a cooperative enterprise is emphasized by the interest in ways of sharing home responsibilities, the care and guidance of children, the management of resources, leisure interests, and community activities. Men as well as women ask for help in preparing for their part as mates and parents.

Of special interest to economists is the fact that how to budget, spend, and save on a very small income are today major issues for young people, who are asking that economic theories shall be translated in terms of ways to achieve and to protect economic security for self and family. Youth wants to understand the issues involved when the wife is employed, factors to consider in assuming and retiring debts, and how much it costs for two to live.

There is little interest in the history of the family except as it illuminates the issues of family life today. Young people are more concerned with changing mores as they affect family welfare than with separation and divorce. Consideration of the role of the individual and family in social reconstruction is accepted as a challenge of far greater import than the study of family disintegration.

Young men and women do not ask for ready-made solutions but for a chance to explore the thinking and experience of others in widely separated fields. They want to discuss certain perplexing questions with those who have insight and understanding beyond theirs and to think out their own philosophy and ways of meeting particular problems. If thinking is focused on human relations and interpreted in terms of real experience, many disciplines can make a worth-while contribution to education for marriage and family living.

IMPLICATIONS FOR COLLEGE PROGRAMS OF GUIDANCE AND COUNSELING

The wide range of acute concerns among individuals in any large group emphasizes the need for a personal counseling service, open to all. The conflicts and problems least often expressed may be more vital to the adjustment of the person concerned than all the topics generally considered important for group discussion. The need for psychiatric service and personal counseling is clearly indicated. Opportunities should be provided for the consideration of questions vital to college men and women anticipating or experiencing marriage. Easy access to consultants should be provided by the college.

Perplexities of freshmen with regard to preparation for marriage and present family life adjustments should be considered in planning the orientation program. College freshmen express many anxieties about relationships with other young men and women. Uncertainties about dating, choice of mate, and when to marry are common. Questions concerning adjustments with parents are often acute among first year students. These problems should be considered by advisers and counselors in individual conference and group discussion.

IMPLICATIONS FOR ADULT EDUCATION

Classes and discussion groups dealing with marriage and family living should be available to adults in every community. Since many of the specific concerns of alumni differ markedly from those of undergraduate students, it is assumed that needs and interests change with maturity and experience. College graduates have many questions and anxieties to propose for discussions of satisfying family relations and successful marriage. Classes for young people beyond college age should not, it would seem, be limited to those who are married or engaged, for the concerns of all alumni of from one to five years' standing are quite similar. Since education is recognized as a never-ending process of reorientation in a changing world, there is certainly need of opportunities for adults as well as for youth to continue the study of family adjustment problems.

Bibliography

1. American Association of School Administrators. *Education for Family Life.* Nineteenth Yearbook. Washington, D. C.: American Association of School Administrators, 1941.

2. ANGELL, C. R. *A Study of Undergraduate Adjustment.* Chicago: University of Chicago Press, 1930.

3. BABER, R. E. *Marriage and the Family.* New York: McGraw-Hill Book Co., 1939.

4. ———. "Some Mate Selection Standards of College Students and Their Parents." *Journal of Social Hygiene,* 22 : 115–125, March, 1936.

5. BALDWIN, A. and JOHNSON, M. "Marriage Courses." Washington, D. C.: National Association of Deans of Women, 1939. Mimeographed.

6. BELL, H. M. *Youth Tell Their Story.* Washington, D. C.: American Council on Education, 1938.

7. BIGELOW, M. A. and JUDY-BOND, H. "Courses on Marriage and the Family in Undergraduate Colleges." *Journal of Social Hygiene,* 22 : 25–32, January, 1936.

8. BROMLEY, D. D. and BRITTEN, F. H. *Youth and Sex.* New York: Harper and Brothers, 1938.

9. BURGESS, J. S. *A Joint Course on Marriage and Family Relationships.* Monograph. Published by The Author, Temple University, 1939.

10. BURGESS, H. W. and COTTRELL, L. S. *Predicting Success or Failure in Marriage.* New York: Prentice-Hall, Inc., 1929.

11. BUTTERFIELD, O. M. *Love Problems of Adolescence.* New York: Emerson Books, Inc., 1939.

12. DENNIS, L. T. "The Present Status of the Work in Family Relationships and Child Development Offered in Home Economics Departments in Colleges and Universities." Washington, D. C.: American Home Economics Association, June, 1934. Mimeographed.

13. Educational Policies Commission. *The Purpose of Education in American Democracy.* Washington, D. C.: National Education Association, 1938.

14. FOLSOM, J. K. *The Family.* New York: John Wiley and Sons, Inc., 1934.

15. ———. *Youth, Family and Education.* Washington, D. C.: American Council on Education, 1941.

16. FRANK, LAWRENCE K. "Social Change and the Family." *The Annals of the American Academy of Political and Social Science,* 160 : 94–102, March, 1932.

17. GOODYKOONTZ, B., COON, B. I., and Others. *Family Living and Our Schools.* New York: D. Appleton-Century Co., 1941.

18. GROVES, E. R. "Sex Adjustment of College Men and Women." *Journal of Educational Sociology,* 8 : 353–360, February, 1935.

19. HART, H. "Trends of Change in Textbooks on the Family." *American Journal of Sociology,* 39 : 222–230, September, 1933.

20. HAWORTH, C. E. "Education for Marriage Among American Colleges." *Bulletin of Association of American Colleges,* 21 : 478–481, November, 1935.

21. NEWCOMB, T. "Recent Changes in Attitudes Toward Sex and Marriage." *American Sociological Review,* 2 : 659–667, October, 1937.

22. PETTIT, L. O. and GIBBS, A. *Home Economics Offerings in Institutions of Higher Education, 1932–1933.* Circular 134. Washington, D. C.: U. S. Office of Education. Department of Interior, April, 1934.

23. POPENOE, P. "Mate Selection." *American Sociological Review,* 2 : 735–743, October, 1937.

24. SANDERSON, D. and FOSTER, R. G. "A Sociological Case Study of Farm Families." *The Family,* 11 : 107–114, June, 1930.

24a. SNEDECOR, GEORGE W. *Calculation and Interpretation of Analysis of Variance and Covariance.* Ames, Iowa: Collegiate Press, Inc., 1934.

25. SYMONDS, P. M. *Problems and Interests of Adolescents. Growth and Development: The Bases for Educational Programs.* New York: Progressive Education Association, 1936.

26. TERMAN, L. M. *Psychological Factors in Marital Happiness.* New York: McGraw-Hill Book Co., 1938.

27. WATSON, F. D. "What Some College Men Want to Know About Marriage and the Family." *Social Forces,* 11 : 235–241, December, 1932.

28. WELLS, CARL D. "Courses on 'The Family' in United States Colleges and Universities." Unpublished paper on file, Department of Sociology, University of Chicago, 1926.

29. White House Conference on Child Health and Protection. *Education For Home and Family Life. Part II. In Colleges.* New York: D. Appleton-Century Co., 1932.

30. Work of the Conference. *Living,* p. 25–26. Iowa City, Ia.: The National Conference on Family Relations, January, 1939.

31. ZACHRY, C. B. *Emotion and Conduct in Adolescence.* New York: D. Appleton-Century Co., 1940.

Appendix

PART I

ANALYSIS OF POPULATION TRAITS

To facilitate concise description of the population and to discover variations in traits which might have meaning in the interpretation of responses on other forms, the information given on the personal data form was studied in considerable detail. The findings * helped to determine both population sub-groupings and the need for certain types of statistical analysis.

The young person's satisfaction with his present family life was assumed to have some relationship to his thinking and feeling on questions about marriage and family living. Estimated family income and the occupation and education of each parent gave insight into socio-economic status. Deemed worthy of investigation also were age, marital status, religious affiliation, location of home, and whether the person lived with his family. Information on these and other background traits reported on the personal data form were explored to discover significant likenesses and differences between participants from "S" and "T," between men and women, and between classes.

Age

Information on the age of all freshmen and seniors enrolled at "S" and "T" colleges was obtained from the records of the respective registrars and corrected to the month when responses were obtained. In defining the problem it was assumed that the total experiences of freshmen, seniors, and recently graduated alumni were sufficiently different to warrant consideration of these three groups as separate units. This implied that there are significant differences in chronological age between freshmen and seniors

---

* Tables showing results of tabulation of data and statistical computation are available in the typed copy of this study on file in the Advanced School of Education, Teachers College, Columbia University, New York.

and between seniors and alumni. The assumption was confirmed by the findings, for the differences in mean age between classes were far greater than can be explained by sampling errors alone. The mean age of freshmen participating in the study was 19.16 years, of seniors 21.86 years, and of alumni 24.87 years. These differences in chronological age between freshmen and seniors and between seniors and alumni are significant. Although there seems to be a consistent trend for participants associated with "T" to be younger than those associated with "S," the mean differences in age are significant only between "S" and "T" freshmen.

The mean age of freshman and senior participants from "T" college was compared with the mean age of all freshman and senior students enrolled in the School of Liberal Arts at "T." For freshman and senior subjects from "T" the mean differences in age between participants and their respective class in liberal arts were not significant. In terms of chronological age this sample of undergraduate students from "T" college appears to be representative of the population from which it was selected.

Since data on chronological age of freshmen and seniors in the School of Liberal Arts at "S" were not available, data for all freshman and senior students, a total of 2,396 persons, were used. Significant differences were found between the ages of "S" freshmen and seniors participating in this study and all freshman and senior students enrolled at "S" college. These differences may be associated with the fact that responses were secured from a larger proportion of all liberal arts freshmen and seniors at "T" than of all freshmen and seniors at "S." Whereas 45 per cent (145) of the 321 persons enrolled as freshmen and seniors in the School of Liberal Arts at "T" participated in the study, only 26 per cent (225) of the 880 persons enrolled as freshmen and seniors in the School of Liberal Arts or 8 per cent of all (2,396) freshmen and seniors at "S" participated in the study. The total freshman and senior classes at "S" included many mature students enrolled in technical and professional schools. The selection of the sample deliberately excluded these persons from participation.

Religious Affiliation

Seventy-one per cent of all "S" participants indicated Protestant affiliation, whereas only 37 per cent of all "T" participants were Protestants. Jewish affiliation was claimed by 11.5 per cent of all participants from "S" and 43 per cent of all participants from "T." Fifteen per cent of all "T" participants and 11.5 per cent of all "S" participants indicated Catholic affiliation.

The association of religious affiliation with the college, class, and sex of participants was investigated. The religious affiliations claimed by "T" and "S" freshman and senior subjects were not significantly different from those stated on official registration forms by seniors at "T" and "S" colleges. Therefore, sampling appeared to be fairly representative with regard to this trait.

Although it was not anticipated that the distribution of religious affiliation would vary significantly from class to class within the same college the hypothesis that there was no association between religious affiliation and college class was postulated and the Chi-square Test applied. Separate computations were made for "T" freshmen and seniors, "T" undergraduates and alumni, "S" freshmen and seniors, and "S" undergraduates and alumni. The results indicated that the differences observed could be considered due to chance variations. It can therefore be assumed that there was no association between religious affiliation and college class in the population from which the samples were drawn.

Because there seemed to be a larger proportion of Jewish men than Jewish women at "T," the possibility of association between religious affiliation and sex was explored. Data from undergraduate and alumni participants from "S" consistently point to lack of association between religious affiliation and sex. A different situation was evident for participants from "T." The largest single group of "T" men (75 persons or 48 per cent) claimed Jewish affiliation. The hypothesis that there is no association between religious affiliation and sex in the population from which all "T" participants were drawn was rejected. Further analysis indicated that the small variation with respect to religious affiliation among "T" senior men and women may be ascribed to sampling error but the variations among "T" freshman men and women were significantly great. The reasons for this difference between classes at "T" are not known.

Marital Status

As could be expected in a group where more than half were freshmen and fewer than one in four were alumni, most of the subjects were not married. Of the total group participating in the study, 39 were married, 53 were engaged to be married, and 538 were single and not engaged. Only two freshmen and two seniors were married. All four were men. Eleven out of 320 freshmen and 26 out of 164 seniors were engaged. The proportion of undergraduates participating in the study who indicated that they were engaged was approximately the same in the "S" and "T" groups, 8 per cent of

"S" undergraduates and 9 per cent of "T" undergraduates. Of the 148 alumni, 35 were married and 16 were engaged. This group of 51 represented 39 per cent of "S" alumni and 24 per cent of "T" alumni who participated in the study.

Location of Present Home

"T" is located in a city with a population close to two million and "S" is located in a town with a population of more than six thousand. Most of the "T" freshmen and seniors come from homes in large cities. Sixty-nine per cent of participating "T" undergraduates indicated that their home was located in a city with a population over 100,000. Many "T" students live with their families in and near the large city in which "T" is located. Only 22 per cent of the "S" freshman and senior students participating in the study come from homes in cities with a population over 100,000. These cities are located more than 100 miles distant from the town in which "S" is located. Approximately half (51 per cent) of "S" freshman and senior students come from homes in cities with a population between 2,500 and 100,000. Only two of these cities, both under 10,000 population, are within a radius of 25 miles of "S." Trains carrying passengers do not serve the town in which "S" is situated. Transportation facilities are limited so that few "S" students with homes outside the college town travel daily between home and college. Many students go home only three or four times each year, usually during the regular college vacations. Twenty-four per cent of the "S" freshman and senior students as contrasted with 11 per cent of "T" freshman and senior students indicated that their homes are located in towns under 2,500 population. Only fourteen "S" undergraduates and two "T" undergraduates checked "farm" as the location of their present home.

The Chi-square Test was applied to investigate association of home location with college, class, and sex. Farm and town groups were combined to form one category in the computations. The results of the Chi-square Test indicate that the differences between the location of homes of "T" and "S" subjects are significant. College class and location of present home, however, do not seem to be associated. The largest chi-square obtained in testing association between location of present home and college class referred to undergraduate students and alumni at "S." Since this chi-square (8.24) has a probability value between $P_{.02}$ and $P_{.01}$ it suggests that there may be some association, although it is open to question. The tendency of alumni to go to cities seeking employment may be a factor related to the larger proportion of city homes indicated by this group. Forty per cent of all undergraduates had homes in cities over 100,000 as contrasted with 46 per cent of all alumni.

No association has been demonstrated in this study between location of home and sex. The greatest difference was observed between senior men and senior women, the men more frequently coming from larger cities. Eighteen out of 103 senior men (17 per cent) and 18 out of 58 senior women (31 per cent) indicated their home was located in a farm or town. Twenty out of 58 senior women (34 per cent) and 56 out of 103 senior men (54 per cent) indicated that home was located in a city with a population over 100,000. However, the chi-square obtained in testing the significance of the differences between senior men and senior women is small enough to indicate that there is doubt concerning association between location of home and sex.

Where Participants Lived at the Time of the Study

In view of the locations of "T" and "S" colleges and of the homes of the participants, it would be reasonable to expect that many "T" freshmen and seniors live at home and many "S" freshmen and seniors live away from home. Of "T" undergraduates participating in the study 38 (78 per cent) reported that they lived at home or with relatives while attending college, whereas only 23 (7 per cent) "S" undergraduates lived with members of the family throughout the academic year. Ten per cent (17) of "T" undergraduate students stated that they lived in dormitories, fraternity or sorority houses as contrasted with 62 per cent (192) of "S" undergraduate students. One factor pertaining to the difference in place where participants lived at the time of the study may be availability of accommodations in dormitories and fraternity and sorority houses associated with the two colleges. In 1936–37 dormitories maintained by "T" housed 150 women students. "T" maintains no dormitories for men. In the same year "S" maintained dormitories housing 288 men students and 820 women students. The personnel deans at "T" and "S" respectively estimated that fraternity and sorority houses in 1936–37 provided accommodations for approximately 75 men and 65 women at "T," and 1,450 men and 80 women at "S." The very large chi-square indicates that the hypothesis that there is no association between college attended and place of abode could not be accepted.

It can be assumed that there is no association between place of abode and college class except for "S" undergraduates and "S" alumni. The differences between where "S" undergraduate students lived at the time of the study and where "S" alumni students lived are significant. This seems reasonable since 62 per cent of the "S" undergraduates participating in the study stated that they lived in a dormitory, or in fraternity or sorority houses. Seventy-five "S" alumni (77 per cent) lived with their families. There is reason to believe that there is no association between place of abode and sex with reference to the alumni of the two colleges. This is not true for undergraduates. Only seven undergraduate women were boarding as contrasted with 107 undergraduate men. A smaller proportion of undergraduate men (56 per cent) than of women (77 per cent) at "S" lived in dormitories, or in fraternity and sorority houses. Only 5 per cent of the "T" undergraduate men and 22 per cent of the "T" undergraduate women participating in the study lived in dormitories, or in fraternity or sorority houses. Both institutions discourage young women students from boarding with persons other than relatives or persons approved by the college.

Occupation of Parents

As one index to family socio-economic status, information concerning the occupation of each parent during the major part of the preceding five years was sought. Responses were tabulated in terms of the classification of occupations used in the Fifteenth Census of the United States, 1930. To simplify analysis certain groups of occupations considered in the census tabulation as separate units were combined in this study. The categories used for tabulating occupation of father were: (1) agriculture, forestry and fishing; (2) mineral, manufacturing, and mechanical industries; (3) trade, transportation, and communication; (4) professional services; and (5) public, domestic, and personal services. The same categories were used in the analysis of occupation of mother except that homemaking was added as a sixth category. Where no occupation was listed for the mother, it was assumed she was a homemaker. Where homemaking and an occupation other than homemaking were reported, only the occupation other than homemaking was tabulated.

In rank order from greatest to least frequency, the number of fathers in each occupational group were: (1) trade, transportation, and communication; (2) mineral, manufacturing, and mechanical industries; (3) professional services; (4) agriculture, forestry, and fishing; and (5) public, personal, and domestic services. Thirty-eight per cent of all fathers were reported as engaged in trade, transportation, and communication. In similar rank order the occupations of mothers were: (1) homemaking; (2) trade, transportation and communication; (3) professional services; (4) mineral, manufacturing, and mechanical industries; (5) public, personal, and domestic services; and (6) agriculture, forestry, and fishing. Nine out of every 10 mothers were occupied as homemakers during the major part of the preceding five years.

A larger proportion of fathers of "T" undergraduates (49 per cent) than of fathers of "S" undergraduates (38 per cent) were engaged in trade, transportation, and communication. Only 7 per cent of "S" fathers and 3 per cent of "T" fathers were engaged in agriculture, forestry, and fishing. These are reasonable findings in view of the greater concentration of "T" families in urban communities. There is reason, however, to doubt the significance of the difference in the total occupational distribution of fathers in the population from which "T" and "S" subjects were drawn. The results of the Chi-square Test indicate lack of association both between father's occupation and college and between father's occupation and class of the participant.

Except for "S" undergraduate men and women there seems to be no association between occupation of father and sex of the participant. The relatively large proportion of "S" undergraduate women (31 per cent) as contrasted to men (12 per cent) who reported fathers engaged in the professions probably contributed to the significant differences in distribution of father's occupation between men and women undergraduate students at "S."

Only 64 mothers out of 632 were reported to have an occupation other than homemaking. Thirteen out of 29 "S" mothers with occupations other than homemaking were engaged in professional services. Taken as a whole, the distribution of mothers' occupations probably does not differ significantly between colleges or between men and women in the population from which these samples were drawn.

Occupations other than homemaking were recorded for 11 per cent of the mothers of freshmen, 10 per cent of the mothers of seniors, and 7 per cent of the mothers of alumni. These differences in percentage are not significant. The ratio of the difference in per cent to the standard deviation of the difference is 0.50 for freshmen versus seniors, and 0.73 for seniors versus alumni.

Education Completed by Parents

There is no association between education completed by the father and college of the participant. Ninety fathers of "T" subjects completed the eighth grade, 66 fathers completed high school, and 48 fathers completed college. Among "S" fathers 118 completed the eighth grade, 146 completed high school, and 129 completed college. Fathers of "T" and "S" freshmen appeared to differ more in the amount of schooling completed than the entire group of "T" and "S" fathers. The differences between the amounts of education completed by fathers of freshmen at "T" and "S" were such that the chi-square was close to the critical point. While about the same proportion of "T" and "S" fathers of freshmen (40 per cent and 41 per cent respectively) had completed high school, only 18 per cent of "T" fathers as compared with 32 per cent of "S" fathers had completed college.

Apparently there is no association between education completed by the father and college class. Variations between the amount of education completed by fathers of freshmen and seniors at the two institutions were small enough to be explained as fluctuations in sampling. Even with undergraduates and alumni the differences are too small to be considered significant. The hypothesis that there is no association between father's occupation and college class was accepted.

The undergraduate women at the two institutions indicated that 40 per cent (52) of their fathers had completed college and 22 per cent (23) of their fathers had completed the eighth grade but not high school. Only 25 per cent (82) of the fathers of undergraduate men had completed college as compared to 36 per cent (121) of their fathers who had completed the eighth grade but not high school. The Chi-square Test indicated that the differences in education completed by fathers of freshman and senior men and freshman and senior women were significant. A longer period of education and the greater incidence of professional work suggests that undergraduate women may come from families with higher socio-economic status than undergraduate men. The differences between the amounts of education completed by fathers of alumni men and women were not significant.

The same general relationships between education completed by the mother and the college, college class, and sex of the participant are apparent. No significant difference in the amount of schooling completed by the mother was evident between "T" and "S" seniors or "T" and "S" alumni. As observed with fathers, mothers of "S" freshmen had completed significantly more schooling than mothers of "T" freshmen. Forty-six per cent of mothers of "T" freshmen and 22 per cent of mothers of "S" freshmen had completed the eighth grade but not high school. Seven per cent of mothers of "T" freshmen and 27 per cent of mothers of "S" freshmen had completed college. However, the Chi-square Test indicated no association between the amount of schooling completed by the mother and the college class of the participants.

Considered as a whole, the association between the amount of education completed by the mother and the sex of the participant is open to question. While there seems to be no association between education of mothers and sex of undergraduate participants, this is not true for alumni men and women. Here again the mothers of men seem to have had less education than the mothers of women. Fifty per cent of the mothers of men of the classes of 1932 to 1936 inclusive had completed less than high school as contrasted with 20 per cent of the mothers of women graduated in the same classes.

Estimated Family Income for the Past Year

Freshmen, seniors, and alumni were asked to indicate by a check mark the approximate income of the family during the preceding year. That it was more difficult for freshmen than for seniors and alumni to make an estimate is indicated by the fact that 25 freshmen as compared with three seniors and two alumni failed to respond. Some participants gave a guess based on relatively limited information and understanding. It is possible that a tendency to exaggerate family income operated throughout. The chi-square technique was applied to test association of estimated family income with the college, class, and sex of the participant. In the computations estimated incomes over $5,000 were grouped in one category and unknown incomes were omitted.

The hypothesis that there is no association between family income and college was accepted for seniors and alumni but rejected for freshmen and for the total group. According to the estimates made by students the incomes of families of "S" freshmen tend to be higher than the incomes of the families of "T" freshmen. Estimates made by participants indicated that 9 per cent of families of "S" freshmen and 21 per cent of families of "T" freshmen received a total income under $1,500. Twenty-seven per cent of the families were judged to have received an income over $5,000 for the year preceding the study.

The hypothesis that there is no association between estimated family income and college class seemed reasonable and was accepted when subjected to the Chi-square Test. There is reason to believe that family income is not associated with sex of "S" participants. The hypothesis that there is association between family income and sex with respect to "T" subjects is accepted with misgivings. Women from "T" tended to give a higher estimate of family income than men from "T." The variation may be related to errors in estimates rather than to real differences. However, it is interesting to recall that fathers of "T" women had completed significantly more education than fathers of "T" men.

Rating of Present Family Life

Freshmen, seniors, and alumni were asked to check one of seven lists of words describing different degrees of satisfaction with present family life. The first word in each list, namely, ideal, successful, satisfactory, indifferent, unsatisfactory, unsuccessful and breaking, was considered descriptive of the unit on the scale. It is not assumed that units on the rating scale are unique or equidistant. Reliability and validity of the scale were assumed, not established by investigation. Undergraduate students did not seem to find the scale too difficult to use, for all but one senior gave a rating. Sixteen alumni failed to give ratings, some stating that they could claim no family life at present because of prolonged absence from home or because their families were broken by death. The difficulty of making an unbiased estimate, and unwillingness to acknowledge or reveal less than complete satisfaction with family life probably influenced ratings. It is probable that this halo effect operated throughout to present favorable ratings. The chi-square technique was used to test hypotheses concerning lack of association between rating of family life and other traits judged to be germane to the problem. Because of the relatively small number of cases where family life was rated indifferent, unsatisfactory, unsuccessful or breaking, these categories were combined to form one category in the computations.

Seventeen per cent (108) of all participants who rated their present family life considered it ideal, 36 per cent (227) successful, 32 per cent (195) satisfactory, 5 per cent (29) indifferent, 7 per cent (35) unsatisfactory, and 3 per cent (21) unsuccessful or breaking.

Results of the Chi-square Test indicate that there is probably no association between rating of family life and college. Freshmen, seniors, and alumni of "S" assigned ratings to their present family life which did not differ significantly from ratings assigned by freshmen, seniors, and alumni of "T."

When the ratings assigned to their family life by freshmen and seniors were analyzed significant differences were not found. It is assumed that there probably is no association between rating of family life and college class, considering undergraduates only. However, ratings assigned by alumni, as compared to those given by undergraduates, varied enough to indicate there may be some association between rating and college class if the group as a whole is considered. Only 9 per cent (14) of the alumni rated family life ideal, as contrasted with 21 per cent (68) of freshmen and 16 per cent (26) of seniors. Fifteen per cent (23) of alumni rated present family life unsatisfactory, unsuccessful or breaking, while only 6 per cent (21) of freshmen and 7 per cent (12) of seniors gave ratings indicating similar dissatisfaction. The less favorable ratings assigned by alumni may be related to the fact that many more alumni than undergraduates were living with relatives. Alumni contacts with family life in the parental home may have been less intimate and perhaps more objectively analyzed.

Alumni men and women varied little in the ratings which they assigned to their family life. While undergraduate men and women differed more than alumni in their ratings, the variations were relatively small and could have arisen in sampling a population in which there was no real difference. There is reason to assume that there is no association between sex and rating of family life.

It is probable that there is no association between religious affiliation and rating of family life except in the case of undergraduate participants from "T" college. The significant differences in ratings by groups with Protestant, Catholic, and Jewish affiliation probably arise from the disparity between ratings assigned by Jewish and non-Jewish participants. Family life was rated ideal by 18 per cent of Jewish and 11 per cent of non-Jewish participants, and indifferent or less by 14 per cent of Jewish and 23 per cent of non-Jewish participants at "T."

Marital status seems to be associated with rating assigned to present family life. Participants who were engaged gave significantly lower ratings to their family life than participants who were not engaged to be married. Only 10 per cent of those who were engaged to be married as contrasted with 19 per cent of those who were single and not engaged rated family life ideal. Twenty-three per cent of those engaged and only 9 per cent of those not engaged rated family life unsatisfactory, unsuccessful or breaking. The hypothesis that there is no association between marital status and ratings assigned by 22 married participants and 62 engaged participants was tested and accepted. Married and engaged participants assigned to family life in the parental home ratings significantly less favorable than the ratings assigned by single persons who were not engaged to be married.

There seems to be no association between the place of abode of undergraduate students and their rating of family life. However, there is reason to believe that association exists between ratings given and whether alumni lived in their own or the parental home. Sixty persons who lived in homes other than the parental home gave ratings both to their own present family life and to that in the parental home. This group included 22 who were married. Participants living in homes other than the parental home rated their own family life significantly higher than that in the parental home.

It is interesting that there is no evidence to indicate an association between unfavorable rating of family life and the fact that the mother has an occupation other than homemaking.

The evidence that there is no association between rating of family life and estimated family income is accepted with some misgiving. The lack of association indicated by the chi-square based on the four levels of income is further questioned in the light of significant differences in rating of family life by those with income under \$1,500 and over \$5,000. The Chi-Square Test applied to these extreme groups indicated that it is reasonable to believe that the rating of family life and family income are associated. Of the 81 persons estimating family income to be less than \$1,500, only 13 per cent rated family life ideal and 23 per cent rated it less than satisfactory.

Separated and Divorced Parents

Only 15 undergraduates and four alumni indicated that parents were separated or divorced.

Certain College Courses Taken

Although at the time of the study no participants were enrolled in sociology courses dealing primarily with the family or family relations, some indicated that they had taken college courses in sociology, family relationships, and home economics at an earlier date. Sociology courses had been taken by 272 participants, family relationships by 61, and home economics by 42. Results of the Chi-Square Test indicate that there probably is association between courses taken, college, and college class. A smaller proportion of "S" than "T" undergraduates had taken courses in sociology. Only 29 of the 272 subjects who had taken courses in this field were freshmen. More "S" than "T" students had taken college courses in home economics. Nineteen of the 42 persons who had taken courses in home economics were freshmen, 17 of these being "S" freshman women. These differences are probably related to variations in curriculum requirements in the two institutions.

There is no reason to believe that there is association between courses taken and sex. Both men and women had taken courses in home economics and family relationships as well as in sociology. The data indicate relatively little difference in the distribution of courses taken by men and by women in the three specified areas. The chi-square obtained indicates that the differences observed are probably not significant.

Membership in Discussion Group

Of the 605 persons who responded to the question "Do you belong to or attend fairly often any group in which problems of human relations are discussed?" 188 answered "yes" and 417 answered "no." The hypothesis that there is no association between college and membership in a discussion group was accepted with misgiving. The fact that 21 per cent of "T" freshmen and 36 per cent of "S" freshmen answered "yes" may reflect a real difference. Living on or near the campus instead of at home may be more conducive to the formation of discussion groups and "bull sessions." There is probably no association between membership in a discussion group and college class or sex.

PART II

OUTLINE FOR THE CLASSIFICATION OF FREE RESPONSE ITEMS IN CATEGORIES

Category I. The Family as a Social Institution

A. Origin and history of marriage and the family
B. The family in society today
  1. The family as a primary or basic social institution
  2. Function of marriage and the family
  3. Relation of the family as an institution to the community
  4. Social problems of the family as an institution
  5. Changing status of women in society

Category II. Two and Three Generation Adjustments

A. Parent-student adjustments
  1. Achieving independence
  2. Confidences, affection between parent and student
  3. Conflict of ideas and standards
  4. Parental control of boy-girl relationships and behavior
  5. Obligations of youth to parents
  6. Parent role in choice of vocation
B. Adjustments to relatives after marriage
  1. When and how to live with family after marriage
  2. Obligations to relatives

Category III. Premarriage Problems *

A. Whom to marry
  1. Who should and should not marry
  2. How to choose a mate, including role of: (a) heredity, health, and physical qualities; (b) education and intellectual level; (c) social status and background; (d) likes, dislikes, and interests; (e) personality; (f) religion, race, and nationality; (g) age differential; (h) infatuation, love; (i) how to know if choice is the right one.
B. When to marry
  1. Desirable age for marriage
  2. Marriage before or after graduation
  3. Time span between engagement and marriage
  4. Establishment in vocation before marriage
C. Courtship adjustments
  1. Questions to be discussed before marriage
  2. Physical examination before marriage

* See IV-E for premarital sex adjustments and VII-E and G for premarital financial problems.

174

3. How to prepare for marriage
4. Desirable relationships during courtship
D. Youth relationships
    1. How to attract and win regard of other sex
    2. Getting along with other young people
    3. Social life: amount, kind, standards of behavior

CATEGORY IV. SEX

A. General sex education
    1. Amount and kind
    2. Reproduction, anatomy, physiology
B. Sex education of children
C. Venereal disease
D. Psychology of sex
    1. Understanding other sex
    2. Psychology of sex life
E. Premarital sex adjustments
    1. Desirable boy-girl sex relationships
    2. Control of sex impulse of the unmarried
F. Marital adjustments
    1. Sex adjustments in marriage
    2. Childbirth
    3. Extra-marital relations
    4. Importance of sex in marriage
G. Prevention of conception
    1. Techniques of contraception
    2. Ethics of contraception
    3. Spacing of children
H. Prostitution, trial and companionate marriage

CATEGORY V. ACCORD IN FAMILY ADJUSTMENTS *

A. Personal husband-wife relations
    1. Early marriage
    2. Growth of mutual understanding
    3. Confidences, privacy
    4. Permanence of marriage
B. Leisure and outside interests
    1. Shared interests
    2. Outside contacts of individual family members
    3. Family community contacts
C. Psychology of adjustment
    1. Personal and family psychology
    2. Mental hygiene
    3. Personality and character development

* See VIII-C for child's place in the family.

D. General family relations
  1. Family relations, general
  2. Role of tolerance, consideration of others, understanding
  3. Duties and responsibilities of family members
  4. Developing harmony, success, stability
E. Domination and control
  1. Authoritarianism
  2. Democratic adjustment
F. Member role
  1. Parents, adults, youth

CATEGORY VI. DISCORD *

A. Divorce and separation
  1. Divorce and separation, general
  2. Causes
  3. Effects
B. Factors contributing to discord
  1. General causes of discord
  2. Role of specific factors
C. Resolving conflict
  1. Adjustment of conflict
  2. Sources of help in resolving discord

CATEGORY VII. FAMILY ECONOMICS

A. Budgeting
  1. Methods of budgeting
  2. Desirability of budgeting
B. Control
C. Cost of parenthood
  1. Cost of pregnancy
  2. Cost of adequate maintenance of children
D. Savings, insurance, investment
E. General family finance
  1. How to handle family finance
  2. Relation of income to standard of living
  3. Parent-student finances including allowances, support, sacrifices
  4. Importance of money in family life
  5. Financial experience of children and youth
F. Wage-earning wife
  1. Ethics of earning after marriage
  2. Factors influencing desirability
  3. Relation of career to success in marriage
G. Finances to marry
  1. Minimum income needs for marriage

* See IV for suggestions and questions specifically related to sex, accord and discord.

2. Relation of debts and obligations to marriage plans
3. Importance of money in planning to marry

CATEGORY VIII. CHILDREN
A. Physical care
   1. Prenatal care
   2. Care and development of babies and children
   3. Health and minor accidents
B. Guidance
   1. Rearing and guidance of children
   2. Child psychology
   3. Discipline
   4. Allocation of responsibility for guidance
C. Place in the family
   1. When to have children
   2. Role of the child in the family
D. Miscellaneous

CATEGORY IX. RELIGION AND ETHICS
A. Parent-child religious problems including responsibility for child's religious affiliation and education
B. Function in family life
   1. Role of religion in family life
   2. General ethical behavior and values

CATEGORY X. MISCELLANEOUS
A. Homemaking techniques
B. Social behavior
C. Vocations
D. Unclassified

PART III

INQUIRY FORMS

Form A_1

Will You Help?

College students throughout the country are asking for guidance that will help them with the personal problems of family life which confront every college man and woman. They are asking for specific instruction that will point the way to more satisfying family life and to more successful marriage. Several colleges have already developed courses at the request of students. Among them are the University of North Carolina, Purdue University, and Cornell University. Other colleges and universities are seriously considering offering such instruction.

It is difficult for faculty fully to sense the real problems of family adjustment that face college men and women today. Students themselves should help to plan these courses. What do you really want to know? What specific questions would *you* like to have discussed if such a course were to be established at your college? Think it over and make a list of the questions that you, as a student in the proposed course, would like to have included. Write as freely and as frankly as you wish. Do *not* sign your name. The questions will be used impersonally to help other college men and women to get the kind of instruction for which they are asking.

Form B_1

Will You Help?

College students throughout the country are asking for guidance that will help them with the personal problems of family life which confront every college man and woman. They are asking for specific instruction that will point the way to more satisfying family life and more successful marriage. Several colleges have already developed courses at the request of students. Among them are the University of North Carolina, Purdue University and Cornell University. Other colleges and universities are seriously considering offering such instruction.

It is difficult for faculty fully to sense the real problems of family adjustment that face college men and women today. Students themselves should help to plan for the instruction that will be of greatest value to them. In

178

the light of your knowledge of the needs and interests of classmates, what do you believe should be included in such instruction? Think it over and make a list of the specific questions that should be discussed. Write as freely and as frankly as you wish. Do *not* sign our name. The questions will be used impersonally to help college men and women to get the kind of instruction for which they are asking.

Form A₂

Code No._____

College students throughout the country are asking for guidance that will help them with the personal problems of family life that confront every college man and woman. They are asking for specific instruction that will point the way to more satisfying family life now and to more successful marriage. Many prominent colleges are offering or planning to offer such instruction. They need to know what college students themselves consider important questions to be included if the instruction is to be most helpful.

What questions do you believe should be included if such instruction were to be offered at your college? On what questions concerning family life do you and your classmates really need and want help?

Think it over and suggest some very specific questions that honestly express *what you really want*. Write as freely and as frankly as you can. Do *not* sign your name. The questions that you suggest will be used impersonally to help other college men and women.

Form A₃

Code No._____

There is a general movement among colleges today to offer to their students guidance in personal problems and family relationships. Because of our interest in the movement we are asking you, as an alumnus, to give suggestions as to the kind of guidance you feel would be most helpful. What should college men and women be taught in order that they may make the decisions and adjustments which will contribute to happy and successful family life?

Just what, in your opinion, should young men and women know to fit them for their roles in family life, as sons and daughters, brothers and sisters, husbands and wives, fathers and mothers? What questions should they think through? What problems should be discussed? What have you been forced to learn from experience that could have been learned in college? In the light of your personal experience, won't you make your suggestions?

Do not sign your name. Our interest is wholly impersonal. We ask only that you state frankly what guidance you think should be given college men and women today in order that they may more successfully meet the every-day problems of family living.

Form C₁

Code No.—————

Listed below are a number of topics suggested by college students as desirable content for instruction concerning marriage and family life. Read through the whole list and cross out any topic that you do not understand. Then go back and rate each topic according to the relative value of such instruction in helping young people to meet more intelligently the personal problems of family life that you and your classmates experience. Give a rating to each topic in the column "Value to You" and also in terms of "Value to Others."

Circle V if you consider the topic of VERY GREAT value.
Circle M if you consider the topic of MODERATE value.
Circle L if you consider the topic of LITTLE value.
Circle O if you consider the topic of NO value.

Value to You Personally					Value to Others			
V	M	L	O	Budgeting the income	V	M	L	O
V	M	L	O	The place of religion in family life	V	M	L	O
V	M	L	O	How to bring up children	V	M	L	O
V	M	L	O	The actual causes of marriage failure	V	M	L	O
V	M	L	O	Specific sex information	V	M	L	O
V	M	L	O	The history of the family in western civilization	V	M	L	O
V	M	L	O	Factors to be considered in deciding when to marry	V	M	L	O
V	M	L	O	Laws affecting family life	V	M	L	O
V	M	L	O	Relation of parental control to youth's desire for independence	V	M	L	O
V	M	L	O	Function of the family in society today	V	M	L	O
V	M	L	O	Sex education of children	V	M	L	O
V	M	L	O	Boy-girl social relations while in college	V	M	L	O
V	M	L	O	Adjusting to old fashioned family attitudes	V	M	L	O
V	M	L	O	Early marital adjustments	V	M	L	O
V	M	L	O	Problems to be jointly discussed before marriage	V	M	L	O

Value to You Personally					Value to Others			
V	M	L	O	Family life in primitive cultures	V	M	L	O
V	M	L	O	Practical problems in homemaking	V	M	L	O
V	M	L	O	Brother-sister relations	V	M	L	O
V	M	L	O	Wholesome sex adjustments of the unmarried	V	M	L	O
V	M	L	O	Physical care of young children	V	M	L	O
V	M	L	O	Youth's responsibility to his family after 21	V	M	L	O
V	M	L	O	Adjustments to in-laws and relatives	V	M	L	O
V	M	L	O	Birth control	V	M	L	O
V	M	L	O	Marriage and career	V	M	L	O
V	M	L	O	The future of the family in America	V	M	L	O
V	M	L	O	Personality adjustments of husband and wife	V	M	L	O
V	M	L	O	Ways of solving modern marriage problems	V	M	L	O
V	M	L	O	Personality development of children	V	M	L	O
V	M	L	O	Pros and cons of divorce	V	M	L	O
V	M	L	O	Qualifications to consider in choosing a mate	V	M	L	O

Form C_2

Code No._____

Listed below are a number of questions concerning marriage and family life which students have suggested as important for college instruction.

1. Read through the whole list and cross out any question that you do not understand.

2. Go back and rate each question on the basis of its value to YOU personally as a subject for discussion. Would these discussions help you to meet more intelligently your personal problems of family life?

Circle 1 if you consider discussion of the question of VERY GREAT value to you.
Circle 2 if you consider discussion of the question of GREAT value to you.
Circle 3 if you consider discussion of the question of MODERATE value to you.
Circle 4 if you consider discussion of the question of LITTLE value to you.
Circle 5 if you consider discussion of the question of NO value to you.

VALUE TO YOU PERSONALLY					
V.G.	GR.	MOD.	LIT.	NO	
1	2	3	4	5	How can a young person make himself more popular with other young people?
1	2	3	4	5	How can conflicting personalities in the family be brought into harmony?
1	2	3	4	5	How does an understanding of the historical development of the family help the individual to adjust more successfully to new trends in family life today?

VALUE TO YOU PERSONALLY

V.G.	GR.	MOD.	LIT.	NO	
1	2	3	4	5	Exactly what should young people know about the anatomy and physiology of normal sex life?
1	2	3	4	5	Does a wife's career, continued after marriage, tend to solve or give rise to more problems?
1	2	3	4	5	How shall a compromise be effected between husband and wife when both desire to dominate?
1	2	3	4	5	What is the responsibility of the family for the religious life of its members?
1	2	3	4	5	By what means can parents and older brothers and sisters be brought to recognize the maturing abilities of the 'teen age young person?
1	2	3	4	5	As family responsibilities pile up, how may personal interest in one another be sustained by husband and wife?
1	2	3	4	5	What factors should be considered when choosing a mate?
1	2	3	4	5	In view of present social and economic trends what kind of family life will probably meet the needs of society in 1957?
1	2	3	4	5	What part should small children play in the life of the family group?
1	2	3	4	5	What are the arguments for and against birth control?
1	2	3	4	5	Is it possible to trace the most common difficulties of marriage to weaknesses in the family system?
1	2	3	4	5	How can natural sex drives of youth be directed when marriage must be delayed?
1	2	3	4	5	How shall mutual satisfaction be achieved by husband and wife in the disposition of their leisure time?
1	2	3	4	5	To what extent does religion contribute to success in marriage?
1	2	3	4	5	From the point of view of society as a whole what are the arguments for and against divorce?
1	2	3	4	5	What adjustments may be made in courtship that will contribute to success in marriage?
1	2	3	4	5	When young people have been accustomed to much at home, are they wise to risk marriage on a small income?
1	2	3	4	5	To what extent is success in marriage dependent upon the satisfactory adjustment of sex needs between husband and wife?
1	2	3	4	5	How may a just division of a small income be made to meet family needs?
1	2	3	4	5	How do the early childhood experiences influence the development of a child's personality?

VALUE TO YOU PERSONALLY
V.G.   GR.   MOD.   LIT.   NO.

V.G.	GR.	MOD.	LIT.	NO.	
1	2	3	4	5	How does one free himself, without quarreling, from excessive family domination?
1	2	3	4	5	Exactly what should every young man and girl know about child care and child psychology?
1	2	3	4	5	While financially dependent upon one's family, is the college man or girl justified in opposing parents in matters of religion, behavior, politics, and so forth?
1	2	3	4	5	What are the most common causes of marriage failures?
1	2	3	4	5	Just how great a hazard is difference of religion in establishing lasting harmony in marriage?

General Information Form

Code No._____

Your name should NOT appear on this page.

The information requested on this sheet will be considered strictly confidential and anonymous. Your frank and complete co-operation is asked to make it of greatest value. Where choices are given, please check (X) the proper response. Fill in other spaces.

1. Man_____. Woman_____. Age at last birthday_____. Present occupation_____.
2. I have completed one_____, 2_____, 3_____, 4_____, 5_____, 6_____years of college work.
3. Course or major subject in college_____.
4. Religious affiliation: Protestant_____, Catholic_____, Jewish_____, Other_____, None_____.
5. I am now married_____, engaged to be married_____, single, not engaged to be married_____.
6. Location of childhood home: Farm_____, town up to 2500_____, small city _____, city over 100,000_____.
7. Location of present home: Farm_____, town up to 2500_____, small city_____, city over 100,000_____.
8. I am now living at home_____, in dormitory_____, elsewhere (specify)_____.
9. My parents are both living_____, mother only living_____, father only living _____, both dead_____.
10. My parents are living together_____, separated_____, divorced_____.
11. Occupation of father during major part of last five years_____.
12. Occupation of mother during major part of last five years_____.
13. Schooling completed by father: 8th grade_____, high school_____, college_____.
14. Schooling completed by mother: 8th grade_____, high school_____, college_____.
15. Number of older brothers and sisters_____. Number of younger brothers and sisters_____.

16. Check the group of words, given below, which most nearly characterizes your present family life. Use the series of adjectives merely as a guide for placing your check.

_____Ideal—devoted, harmonious, sympathetic, co-operative, loyal, happy.

_____Successful—affectionate, united, considerate, contented, peaceful, understanding.

_____Satisfactory—friendly, easy-going, complacent, steady, conciliatory, tolerant.

_____Indifferent—unconcerned, individualistic, unco-operative, disinterested, thoughtless.

_____Unsatisfactory—dissatisfied, restless, worried, critical, sarcastic, unsympathetic.

_____Unsuccessful—discordant, unhappy, quarrelsome, unfriendly, intolerant, nagging.

_____Breaking—hostile, unforgiving, bitter, antagonistic, disloyal, irreconcilable.

17. When in college did you take courses in sociology_____, Home economics_____, Family relationships_____?

18. When in college to whom would you most likely turn for guidance in personal problems relating to marriage and family life?_____.
If willing, give the person's name_____.

19. Do you belong to or attend fairly often any group in which problems of human relations are discussed?_____yes; _____no.

20. Check the approximate yearly income of your family during the past year.
Under $1,500_____, $1,500 to $3,000_____, $3,000 to $5,000_____, $5,000 to $10,000_____, over $10,000_____.

Supplementary Alumni Information

Some time ago, by filling out and returning certain blanks, you assisted us in a study of family life being conducted in several colleges throughout the country. As this work has progressed, it has been found increasingly interesting and worthwhile. Important new problems have grown out of the original ones which we believe should be studied with the others. However, our data for this is not sufficiently full to permit accurate statistical analysis. With that in mind, we are taking the liberty of presenting to you a third form, partially duplicating the second, but likewise requesting new information. May we ask that you supplement your first response by filling out the following blank. A stamped envelope for its return is enclosed. Thank you.

(Where choices are given, please check (X) the proper response. Fill in other spaces.)

1. Man_____. Woman_____. Age last birthday_____. Present occupation_____.

2. Religious affiliation: Protestant_____, Catholic_____, Jewish_____, Other_____, None_____.

3. I am now married_____, engaged to be married_____, single, not engaged to be married_____.

4. I have completed one_____, 2_____, 3_____, 4_____, 5_____, 6_____years of college work. Degrees_____.

5. Check the group of words, given below, which most nearly characterizes the family life in your parent's home at present:

_____IDEAL—devoted, harmonious, sympathetic, co-operative, loyal, happy.

_____SUCCESSFUL—affectionate, united, considerate, contented, peaceful, understanding.

_____SATISFACTORY—friendly, easy-going, complacent, steady, conciliatory, tolerant.

_____INDIFFERENT—unconcerned, individualistic, unco-operative, disinterested, thoughtless.

_____UNSATISFACTORY—dissatisfied, restless, worried, critical, sarcastic, unsympathetic.

_____UNSUCCESSFUL—discordant, unhappy, quarrelsome, unfriendly, intolerant, nagging.

_____BREAKING—hostile, unforgiving, bitter, antagonistic, disloyal, irreconcilable.

Check the group of words, given below, which most nearly characterizes the family life in your own family life at present:

_____IDEAL—devoted, harmonious, sympathetic, co-operative, loyal, happy.

_____SUCCESSFUL—affectionate, united, considerate, contented, peaceful, understanding.

_____SATISFACTORY—friendly, easy-going, complacent, steady, conciliatory, tolerant.

_____INDIFFERENT—unconcerned, individualistic, unco-operative, disinterested, thoughtless.

_____UNSATISFACTORY—dissatisfied, restless, worried, critical, sarcastic, unsympathetic.

_____UNSUCCESSFUL—discordant, unhappy, quarrelsome, unfriendly, intolerant, nagging.

_____BREAKING—hostile, unforgiving, bitter, antagonistic, disloyal, irreconcilable.

6. Age of husband or wife at last birthday_____.
   Schooling completed by husband of wife: 8th grade_____, high school_____, 2 years of college_____, 4 years of college_____, graduate work_____years. Degrees_____.
   Number of children_____. Ages of children_____.
   Occupation of husband or wife at present is _____.
   Occupation of husband or wife before marriage was_____.
   My wife has not been employed outside the home since marriage_____.
   My wife has been employed continuously outside the home since marriage_____.
   My wife has interrupted her outside employment by periods of remaining at home____.

Form *P₁*

You have very kindly indicated a willingness to cooperate in the study of family life by returning the postal card bearing your signature. We are unable to tell, however, from the card whether you have sent in one or both of the necessary blanks. It is possible the second form (the check list) may not have been received by you. If so, we shall be glad to correct the error by sending the missing blank. Won't you please check and return the attached card? Your cooperation is greatly appreciated.

Return Card

___1. I have returned both blanks.
___2. I have returned only the first letter.
___3. I have returned only the check list.

___4. I am returning the first letter today.
___5. I am returning the check list today.
___6. Please send the first letter___, the check list___, so that I may complete my response.

Signed_____

Form P_2

Have you answered the letter asking for suggestions for instruction in family living? It was mailed to you last week. Since the replies were unsigned, there is no way of telling whose have been received and whose have not. Won't you please check and return the attached card promptly?

Reply Card

1. I have returned the letter to you___.
2. I have not returned it but will do so today___.
3. I would like to reply but have mislaid the letter. Kindly send more blanks___.
4. I am willing to mark a check list if it is mailed to me___.

Your signature is required only for general mailing purposes. No effort will be made to trace identity of any material sent under code number.

Signed_____

Form P_3

We are making a final check on the returns of family life material recently sent to the alumni of Penn State. Won't you please check on the attached card which blanks you have returned? We would appreciate it exceedingly if you would cooperate with us to the finish by returning both forms. Your frank reaction to the subject of family life instruction for college students will be of greatest value to us.

Signed_____

Return Card

1.___I have returned the first letter only.
2.___I have returned the check list only.
3.___I have returned both letter and check list.
4.___I will fill out and send today the blank (or blanks) which I have not yet returned.
5.___Will you please send more blanks? Mine have been mislaid.

Vita

LAURA WINSLOW DRUMMOND was born in Philadelphia, Pennsylvania, August 6, 1901, and received her early education in the public schools of that city. She received the degree of Bachelor of Science from the University of Pennsylvania in 1924, and the degree of Master of Arts from Teachers College, Columbia University in 1926.

She taught home economics in the public schools of Philadelphia and Glenolden, Pennsylvania; and served as instructor of home economics, 1926 to 1930, and as director of home economics 1930 to 1938 at Temple University, Philadelphia. She is now Director of Home Economics at The Pennsylvania State College.

She is a member of Pi Lambda Theta, Kappa Delta Pi, Delta Kappa Gamma, Phi Delta Gamma, and Omicron Nu.